YOUTH-LED DEVELOPMENT

"The concept of youth-led development is quite new, not very well known and without too many warriors fighting for it. So, as a young Activist, I welcome this compelling and passionate defense of it from the man who, more than any other, created and has fought for the idea of YLD. Youth-led development requires a whole cultural shift, not only in the minds of governments and society but – perhaps more important – in youth themselves." – **Marina Marina Mansilla Hermann, Ashoka Youth Venture, Argentina**

"This paper provides a passionate case for supporting Youth-led Development and makes a critical contribution to the field." – **Jennifer Corriero, TakingITGlobal, Canada**

"Convincing – interesting – refreshing – passionate about youth-led development! This paper balances issues with process, highlighting the important and enduring aspects of youth development (education, employment, service) while delving into other areas, like the consolidation of the tax base, effective aid harmonization and security." – **Julie Larsen, UN Youth Unit**

"This short booklet demonstrates that young people are not just tomorrow's leaders, but that they are leading important social change today. Indeed, they are problem solvers, and not the problems which many policy makers label youth today. I salute David Woollcombe, Peace Child International and the many courageous NGOs mentioned here who have been successfully promoting youth leadership and youth-led development for many years now." – **William S. Reese, President & CEO, International Youth Foundation, USA**

Schumacher Briefing No. 14

YOUTH-LED DEVELOPMENT

Empowering youth to make poverty history

David Woollcombe

published by Green Books
for The Schumacher Society

First published in 2007
by Green Books Ltd
Foxhole, Dartington, Totnes,
Devon TQ9 6EB
www.greenbooks.co.uk

for The Schumacher Society
The CREATE Centre, Smeaton Road,
Bristol BS1 6XN
www.schumacher.org.uk
admin@schumacher.org.uk

Printed by TJ International Ltd, Padstow, Cornwall, UK

Text printed on Corona Natural (100% recycled)
Covers and colour plates printed on GreenCoat Velvet (80% recycled)

A catalogue record for this publication
is available from the British Library

ISBN 978 1 903998 98 4

The Schumacher Briefings
Series Editor: Stephen Powell
Founding Editor: Herbert Girardet

Contents

At the World Summit for Sustainable Development in Johannesburg, the Youth Caucus called on us to "see young people as a resource, not a problem". How right they were. Young people are the most precious resource our planet possesses.

Providing for youth is not just a moral obligation, it is a compelling economic necessity. Study after study has shown the benefits to the young and to their communities of investing in education, reproductive health, job skills and employment opportunities for young people.

That is why I have worked to create initiatives such as the Youth Employment Network, set up to fight the tragic waste of youth joblessness. Young leaders of today are vital partners in that effort, and in so many others: eradicating the HIV/AIDS pandemic and other deadly diseases; achieving gender equality and universal primary education for all; and, most importantly, eradicating extreme poverty – the first of the Millennium Development Goals.

In Africa, where I come from, half the children go to bed hungry every night. Many of them lack a bed, some even a roof over their heads. It is hard to imagine, if you have never experienced it, what it is like to be sick and have no doctor to go to, to be hungry and have no food to eat, to want a future but there to be no school to prepare you for it.

With the Millennium Development Goals, the world's governments have committed themselves to halving the number of people living in extreme poverty by 2015. It should be the commitment of your generation to eradicate it completely. It is never too early to be active. If you start young, I am confident that, by the time you are my age, you will succeed. Your generation can Make Poverty History.

Kofi Annan
former Secretary-General, United Nations

List of abbreviations

ABCD – Asset-Based Community Development model

AIESEC – Association Internationale des Etudiants en Sciences Economiques et Commerciales;

AU – African Union

CEDAW – Convention to Eliminate all forms of Discrimination Against Women

CIDA – Canadian International Development Agency

CRC – Convention on the Rights of the Child

DAC – Development Assistance Committee (hosted by the OECD)

DfID – Department for International Development (UK Government's ODA Ministry)

ESD – Education for Sustainable Development

ESL – Education for Sustainable Lifestyles

EVHAC – European Voluntary Humanitarian Assistance Corps

EVS – European Voluntary Service (a programme of the European Union)

FTC – Free the Children

GDP – Gross Domestic Product

GTZ – Deutsche Gesellschaft für Technische Zusammenarbeit *(German Development Agency)*

GYAN – Global Youth Action Network

GYSD – Global Youth Service Day

HDI – Human Development Index

HDR – Human Development Report

IADB – The Inter-American Development Bank

IB – International Baccalaureate

IFF – The International Finance Facility (a programme of the World Bank)

ILO – International Labour Organisation

IT – Information Technology

LDCs – Least Developed Countries

MDG – Millennium Development Goals

MRU – Mano River Union

MRU-YEF - Mano River Union Youth Employment Forum

NGO – Non-Governmental Organisation

ODA – Overseas Development Assistance

ODI – Overseas Development Institute

OECD – Organisation for Economic Cooperation and Development

PRSP – Poverty Reduction Strategy Paper

PT – Prince's Trust

SME – Small to Medium-sized Enterprises

UNDP – United Nations Development Programme

UNFPA – United Nations Population Fund

UNIDO – United Nations Industrial Development Organisation

UN YEN – United Nations Youth Employment Network

USAID – United States Agency for International Development

VISTA – Volunteers in Service for the Americas

VSO – Voluntary Service Overseas

WDR – World Development Report

WYC – World Youth Congress on Youth and Development

YBI – Youth Business International

YLBS-Us – Youth-led Business Start-ups

YLD – Youth-led Development

YLLIIPs – Youth-led Labour-Intensive Infrastructure Projects

YLSEs – Youth-led Social Enterprises

Preface

What a privilege it is to write under the shadow of the name of E. F. Schumacher. If there are any youth drawn by the title of this paper who have yet to read *Small is Beautiful* or *The Guide to the Perplexed* – rush to get your hands on copies before you read another word. Inhale the wisdom of the 20th century's greatest economist never to win a Nobel prize. Or read his last lecture at Caux, which contains the most wonderfully provocative line I have ever read about development: "Overseas development aid is a process where you collect money from the poor people in the rich countries, to give to the rich people in the poor countries." He was very concerned about the economics of development, giving the world the concepts of intermediate technology, 'enoughness' and Buddhist economics. This last he summed up as follows: "Modern economics considers consumption to be the sole end of all economic activity. A Buddhist economist would consider this approach excessively irrational: since consumption is merely a means to human well-being. The aim should be to obtain the maximum of well-being with the minimum of consumption."

His greatest gift was to put flesh on the bones of the idea of 'sustainable development.' He was one of the first to point out that our economy is unsustainable: we are treating natural resources (especially fossil fuels) as expendable income when in fact it should be treated as capital. Long before Stern and others, he was calling on governments to concentrate their investments on creating a sustainable economy because "nature's capacity to resist pollution is limited." More than any other economist, it was Fritz Schumacher who caused a great groundswell of people to rise up and say: 'The purpose of our existence on this earth cannot be to destroy it. Let's reconsider.'

Though my purpose in this paper is to argue the value of Youth-led Development to 'conventional' economists, Schumacher's thought has been a guiding light: in the lifetimes of today's youth, imperatives of sustainability and 'enoughness' will become blindingly obvious to all, and thus 'conventional' wisdom. Many others, young and old, have shaped my thinking on YLD: it is impossible to acknowledge all of them here, but huge thanks to Bill Reese, Andrew Fiddaman, Steve Riffkin, Amy Willsey, Tom

Burke, Rick Little, Ben Quinto, Jennifer Corriero, Marina Mansilla Herman, Alpha Bacar Barry, Jagan Devaraj, Bill Drayton, Fabien Koss, Francisco Pereira, Don Eberly, Steve Culbertson, Werner Greis, Joao Scarpelini, Julie Larsen, Bill Angel, Joop Theunissen, Pat Zakaib, Fred Matser, Richard Jolly, Steven Umemoto, Regina Monticone, Justin Sykes, Asif Hasnain, Juma Assiago, Emmanuel de Casterlé, Driss Guerraoui, Sheku Syl Kamara, Craig Kielburger and Karun Körnig. Any one of them might have made a better fist of this paper than I – but perhaps only I had the arrogance and energy to steal the moments to write it.

And stolen moments they were: I run a small, high pressure, youth-led Development NGO. So this paper was written on the laptop in airports, on the tube, in cafés between meetings (even during the more tedious meetings!). Oh, how I envy you PhD students with your long weeks and months to write your theses – lazy, sun-filled afternoons in libraries checking references. That's not me. I include references here to try to persuade you I have academic credentials (and myself that I didn't make it all up!), but you won't be fooled: at heart, I'm just a true believer making a case.

A case for what, exactly? Young people. I believe that our world would benefit immensely from a more muscular inclusion of young people in our decision-making processes and in the execution of those decisions. Youth-led Development (YLD) is born in the faith that young people can contribute constructively to the good of society in the years before their 25th birthdays. My life is about persuading governments and development agencies to put youth at the heart of their development plans – to empower them to lead, or at least be involved, from an early age in the building of those sustainable economies of which Schumacher dreamed – and on which the lives of my children and their's will depend.

In this, I am supported by the wonderful staff of Peace Child and its Trustees. And my family, Rosey, Alexander and Natasha, my co-adventurers on the Peace Child journey – my sternest critics and my greatest friends, without whom my faith in young people would never have made it out of the starting gate.

David R. Woollcombe,
Buntingford, July 2007

Executive summary

The Hypothesis

Youth-led Development (YLD) is the best investment anyone can make in development. In its 2007 World Development Report, 'Development and the Next Generation', the World Bank does not mention YLD. However, by focusing on youth issues in its major annual review, the Bank shone a powerful spotlight on the youth development sector. The report concludes: "There has never been a better time to invest in youth . . .",[1] and lays out compelling reasons for why this is so.

The purpose of this paper is to expand on those arguments to persuade governments, especially donor governments, and those of Least-Developed Countries (LDCs), that putting youth at the heart of their development policies makes sense for many reasons. Demographics for one: with young people under the age of 25 forming 60-70 percent of LDCs' population,[2] logic dictates that they should have a central role. There are many other strong reasons why YLD represents an irresistible proposition to all governments:

First – the importance of learning by doing

Study after study has proved that experiential education beats classroom-based, cognitive education as the most effective means of imparting information to young people.[3] YLD is essentially learning by doing: young people learning to flex their entrepreneurial muscles by starting up a small business to deliver a product or a service; or learning about project management – budgeting, scheduling, team-building and staff management etc. – by running a small community-improvement project. These projects teach young people skills essential to their later employability. They build young people's self-esteem and self-confidence, improve their social attitudes and strengthen civil society. Governments invest heavily in schools to impart knowledge and skills. This paper urges governments to invest in YLD for the same reason.

Second – sustainable jobs

Youth-led Development helps create sustainable jobs. Decent, dignified jobs for young people: jobs in the private sector through Youth-led Business Start-Ups (YLBS-Us); jobs in the public sector and other community infrastructures that teach practical skills at the same time. And jobs in environmental conservation programmes, Youth-led social enterprises (YLSEs), like the proven success of peer-to-peer literacy/teaching projects, HIV-AIDS awareness programmes, etc. All give young people jobs, things to do: things that make them feel wanted, not marginalised, by society. The adult-led approach puts them in an institute, trains them up and sets them loose with a certificate often with zero chance of employment in their chosen trade. Youth-led Development is much more pro-active, holding their hands through actual youth-led business start-ups, supporting them all the way to being successful. In many cases, the adult-led approach simply replaces unskilled unemployed youth with skilled unemployed youth.[4] YLD seeks the creation of decent, safe, sustainable meaningful work for young people – which is the main thing that most of them want.

Third – sustainable economic development

An educated workforce is the single best driver of economic development. Not only does YLD deliver education through peer-to-peer teaching and skills training, it provides the arguably more valuable experiential education as well. Further, by financing YLBS-Us, YLD grows and strengthens the internal markets of LDCs with more products and services, more advertising, more energy in the marketplace and – crucially for government – more tax-payers. YLD is not about putting more hawkers of paper tissues and phone-chargers on the streets of LDC capitals. That is not sustainable economic development. Rather YLD seeks to create formal companies and expand the number of taxpayers.

Fourth – evidence of success

I present compelling evidence of the success of a variety of YLD initiatives – some from my own experience, but mostly from the experience of others. Most young people are refreshingly positive: fun, and full of hope. They carry the aspirations of the planet on their shoulders and they hate to fail. Our YLD approach proposes 'differential mentorship' to provide elder support for young people to be successful. That is the goal of YLD as we perceive it: supporting young people – often living at appalling disadvantage – to succeed in their aspirations and recognise that they have the power to pull themselves out of poverty without waiting around for a government, or a parent, or an international donor to do it for them. Building self-reliance is what YLD does, flagged up in the Gandhi instruction "to be the change you want to see in the world!" – which gave the title to Peace Child's YLD programme.[5]

Fifth – service

Service is an essential component of the YLD ethic – and something that every young person can benefit from doing. More importantly, as proved by the mushrooming numbers of young people in OECD countries eager to volunteer for overseas voluntary service and 'gap years', there is a huge appetite for this.[6] I argue that it should be a part of every young person's formal schooling – on the radar of every student from the moment they enter primary school, and something they look forward to and prepare for throughout their school years. A year in which they consolidate all that they have learned in the schoolroom by using and conveying that knowledge in the field.

I devote a chapter to 'co-management', a technology for 'bridging the generation gap' not much studied in the halls of academe. For YLD, it is crucial: young people must learn that they do not know all the answers. They must be ready to draw on the experience of elders, and elders must learn to stand back and leave ownership of the projects in the hands of the young people doing them.[7] Youth participation sounds simple enough, but there are both good and bad technologies of youth/elder participation. Choosing a good one is critical to the success of any project involving young people.

Sixth – more and better aid

All this adds up to 'More and Better Aid' – as called for in the 2005 Paris Declaration.[8] For implicit in the Paris thinking is 'cost-effectiveness' – saving money. YLD is the most cost-effective form of development known to humanity. The White House Office of Management & Budget website lets slip that "the average cost of putting an American direct hire position overseas in 2006 will be approximately $430,000."[9] That $430,000 invested in the Nationwide YLD Policy, explained in my final chapter, would pay for 18 pairs of local and international volunteers to operate for a year in an LDC – and give each of them a $10,000 fund to invest in YLD projects. This policy has been developed in partnership with young people from some 50 NGOs in West Africa. It seeks to pair local, educated indigenous volunteers with international volunteers to spread out across every town, village and chiefdom of the LDC to seek out, support and invest in small projects costing $500-$1,000, designed and managed by young people of those regions. The International Volunteer brings IT skills plus business and management skills that rub off on both their local volunteer peer and the young people whose business plans and social enterprises they have come to support.

The plan intends to split the investments: 50 percent to YLBS-Us, 50 percent to YLSEs and Youth-led Public Works. Chiefly, it is designed to reach out to every single young person eager to transform their lives within the LDC. In this way, the Nationwide YLD Policy aims to create that critical mass of successful, self-confident young social, commercial and environmental entrepreneurs to cause their LDC nations to leap several tens of places up the UN's Human Development Index (HDI). It is an act of faith, no doubt, to believe that young people can do this where so many others have failed: but this author comes from a background in which youth-led diplomacy created a massive breakthrough in US-Soviet Cold War relations where years of adult-led diplomacy had signally failed.

Finally, in an afterword, I argue that if YLD brings together groups of young volunteers traditionally hostile to each other, to work together in LDCs on simple projects that transform the lives of our planet's most disadvantaged people, they will experience the thrill of unity and learn the imperatives of cooperation, service and sustainable lifestyles essential to our planet's survival. YLD alone will not deliver Schumacher's peaceful, sustainable planet, but it can be a part of the solution. The history of post-World War Two reconstruction, and the ending of the Cold War, teach us that youth exchanges have an important part to play. And they are a whole lot cheaper than most military options.

To summarise: what is the 'ask' here ?

- **ONE:** Put youth at the heart of your development policies. It makes sense;

- **TWO:** Recognise Youth-led Development as a field worthy of exploration;

- **THREE:** Recognise that there's no one right way to do Youth-led Development: therefore test the hypothesis in a number of different ways, to see which way works best for you and for the youth involved. The approach explained in the last chapter of this booklet is just one of several possibilities.

Chapter One

What is Youth-Led Development?

Meet Paula Vika.[1] Paula came to the UK from Angola in September 1999, fleeing from that country's civil war. A single mother, she had a six-year-old daughter. She spoke no English but she was determined to find work to support herself and not rely on handouts.

"My dream was to be an independent hairdresser," she writes, "doing African and European hair styles. But I couldn't get a loan from the banks. I had no references. So I talked to The Prince's Trust. They helped me with a business plan and taught me how to do market research – to see if the business would work. I got out on the street, asking people about their local hairdressers etc. Many seemed excited and interested in my ideas. So the Trust gave me a loan and helped me find a chair at a local salon in Great Yarmouth. Having made a success of that, I was then able, through the Trust, to get a loan and New Entrepreneur Scholarship which helped me to start up my own salon as a European and African hairstylist.

"Before I met The Prince's Trust, no one was helping me. I was struggling. But they gave me a chance to prove what I could do. I now employ two staff. I also train a young girl who comes in on Saturdays and holidays. I think the business has been very good. I pay the rent and the staff. I'm trying to bring in more business, and the salon has a good reputation. I started the business not to be rich, but to work for my daughter and me. To do what I can. If I can do it, anyone can."

Paula is a poster girl for the Prince's Trust[2] – one of over 50,000 young people who have been started in business by Prince Charles' Prince's Trust in the UK. The Prince's Trust is perhaps the earliest, and certainly one of the most successful practitioners of Youth-led Development (YLD): business start-ups or community improvement projects designed and implemented by young people under the age of 25, usually with the help of older mentors. The Trust was started by Prince Charles after he left the Navy in 1972, and it was formally incorporated in 1976. In the Trust, many of the best elements of YLD are well demonstrated. The concept of elders in society 'supporting young people to be successful' is the central element of the Trust's success: their research[3] has found that, where supportive mentors are there for young entrepreneurs, offering them advice and guidance as they start up their businesses, 66% of them are still in business and prospering after three years. Where there are no mentors, the success rates drops to 24 percent.

The Trust's research made another important discovery:[4] it found that one in five young people have the intuitive chutzpah to start and run a small business. And it found that government, and other authorities, currently provide investment funds to only 20 percent of them. The immense contribution that could be made by that other 80 percent of the nation's potential young entrepreneurs is never realised! This inspired Prince Charles to target his Trust's investments on the poor, the unemployed, the disadvantaged, the disabled and the ex-offenders. Many of the Trust's most successful clients have been blind or wheelchair-bound. All of them have been young people whom no one else believed in enough to give them a loan. The Prince's faith in these young people has been repaid many times over. As he wrote to Margaret Thatcher shortly after her re-election in 1987: "I felt very strongly that there is a great deal of hidden, wasted talent in the less prosperous parts of the UK and that it was important to encourage the formation of new enterprises which could, in due course, become major companies."[5] And, in due course, they did: several of the Trust's start-ups are now turning over seven-figure sums. One of the most successful was ATTIK – which became 'Gamestation' and was recently sold for $150m.[6]

Later, the Prince turned his attention to the less prosperous parts of the world and founded Youth Business International – a kind of International Prince's Trust. Remarkably, he found that what was true in the UK was also true in other countries: one in five young people have the intuitive skill to start and run a small business successfully when supported by a caring mentor. YBI's success stories are perhaps even more inspirational than those of the original Trust.

Meet Zablon Muthaka.[7] He lives in the Kangemi slum in Nairobi, Kenya, which has a 40 percent unemployment rate. Observing the heaps of rotting waste in his community and the complete inability of the local municipal authority to deal with it, he spotted a business opportunity and started Beta Bins Waste Management. With a grant from the Kenya branch of YBI and a supportive mentor from the coffee industry, Zablon set about doing market research and perfecting his business plan. With $1,500 start up funds from the Kenya Youth Business Trust, he was able to build a $6,000+ a year business and employ five previously disadvantaged young people. Now, his ambition knows no bounds: "I want to be the Bill Gates of the waste management and environmental conservation industry. Waste is a renewable resource – a source of energy, fertiliser and other raw materials. It just needs Beta Bin Management!" His mentor, Philip Gitou, was also inspired by the experience: "Watching Zablon grow into a real businessman who supports the wider community through the services he provides and the direct employment of disadvantaged young people has made me re-think some of my own business strategies."

Zablon won YBI's Young Entrepreneur of the Year award in 2006 – a $1,500 prize which he plans to invest in new transport for his company. YBI goes from strength to strength, now operating in 39 countries, with a further 20 standing in line to set up their own branches. Will Day of Children in Need commented: "I cannot understand why YBI is not the biggest NGO in the UK. It's brilliant! It provides aid that is not charity – rather direct investment in a nation's economic future. That's the best kind of aid."[8]

Interestingly, while YBI struggles to find funding and grow, the immensely richer Prince's Trust is now winding down its Youth-led Business Start-up operation: youth unemployment has all but ceased to be a problem in the UK. This rather proves the point I am trying to make: that investing in YLD can help turn a whole nation's economy around. Not on it's own, of course: but looking back over the last 30 years of UK history, helping to start and sustain 50,000 new businesses has to have been a contributing factor in the growth and current prosperity of UK Inc.

At the risk of repeating the Executive Summary, let me outline the shape of this Briefing Paper: first, I will outline the history of YLD and my own experience of working with young people – which will help you understand why I am such an enthusiast. I will then explore the three slogans that help define YLD. In Chapter Two, I will explain why investment in YLD represents such an irresistible proposition, and in the next chapter offer irrefutable evidence of its success. In Chapter Four, I discuss the extraordinary history of youth service. YLD is essentially another way of describing this kind of service that has supported governments and communities down the centuries. In Chapter Five, I explain how governments and other institutions can bring youth into decisions that affect them. I highlight 'Co-Management' technology, which offers an important foundation for successful Youth-led Development. In Chapter Six, I offer a policy for Nationwide Youth-led Development, designed to impact every young person in three countries in West Africa.

As a taxpayer, as much as a development theorist, I make the case for Youth-led Development as I believe it is the best possible use of taxpayers' money. The logic of investing in YLD seems to me to be inescapable. However, it is a logic that has so far escaped the minds of most of the major government overseas development ministries and largest development NGOs. I do not intend to dwell on my frustrations and as-yet-unsuccessful efforts to persuade the mandarins of the development industry of the massive potential of YLD. However, in pursuit of 'More and Better Aid', an essential context for this Briefing is that much of current aid policy not only does not work; in many parts of Africa it has led to corrosive dependency which has caused some economies to lurch into reverse in recent years. There has to be a better way to do development. YLD is one part of that better way. And this paper sets out to prove why.

The fault does not just lie with the blindness of overseas development ministries. Most developing country governments know that they are failing their youth and are struggling to do something about it. Several have produced impressive National Youth Policies and Youth Employment Action Plans, but when it comes to budgets few, if any, have attached serious funding to these policies. The UN's Youth Employment Network has done impressive research in West Africa that confirms this impression. [See table on facing page].[9]

Similar research would produce similar results for most of the developing countries in which we have worked. This is the situation that has to change if that great engine of massed young people is to be fired into life. Once that engine is firing on all cylinders – well oiled, fuelled and motivated – the changes will start to come very rapidly. Of that I am absurdly confident. The reasons for my confidence are rooted in the experience of a career spent working with young people to address global challenges.

So, though there is much to regret in government and institutional indifference to the needs and the potential of young people, in this Briefing I want to accentuate the positive; to focus on celebrating the achievements of some magnificent young people, some of whom operate in circum-

Youth Employment Policy
& Budgets Data in the UNOWA region

COUNTRY	Youth Employment Policy?	Budget Assigned?	Notes
Benin	No	Nothing	- 0 -
Burkina Faso	No	Funds Promised not delivered	Budget: youth promotion, credit & training;
Cap Verde	No	Nothing	- 0 -
Cote D'Ivoire	YES	Some	$130m for private sector Youth Employment
The Gambia	YES	Nothing	- 0 -
Ghana	YES	Some	$140m broadly for "Other poverty Exp."
Guinea	No	Some	Tech. & Vocational Education: $2.2m
Guinea-Bissau	No	Nothing	- 0 -
Liberia	YES	Nothing	Liberia Emergency Emp Prog seeks funds
Mali	YES	Nothing	Ambitious Programme No funding!
Mauritania	No	Some	Tech. & Vocational Education: $1.3m
Niger	No	Nothing	- 0 -
Nigeria	No	Nothing	- 0 -
Senegal	YES	Some	$6.7m for Ed. & Train; $1m for micro-credit
Sierra Leone	YES	Funds Promised not delivered	$4.5m UNDP fund + $9m PBC; none spent
Togo	No	Nothing	- 0 -
TOTALS	**9 x No** **7 x Yes**	**9 x Nothing** **7 x Some / promise**	

stances of appalling disadvantage. I hope that by drawing attention to their achievements – and their incredible skills, energy and commitment – governments will wake up to the idea that young people are excellent partners in their efforts to achieve their wider development goals, and that a focus on youth should be at the heart of their development policy.

Young people themselves articulated their 'ask' to governments and all overseas development agencies at the second World Youth Congress (WYC) on Youth-led Development in Morocco in 2003: "We appeal to government development ministries and UN agencies to devote 0.7 percent of their annual budgets to projects designed, managed, and implemented by young people."[10] The same ask was repeated at the next WYC in 2005. This 0.7 percent for 51 percent of the world's population doesn't seem too much to ask. But when the request was sent to the world's major development agencies, not one of them was prepared event to sit down and discuss it. That is the mountain which we advocates of YLD have set out to climb.

The history of YLD and the Asset-based approach to Youth in Development

There will always be arguments as to who used the phrase, 'Youth-led Development' first. I first heard it in a speech to the Millennium Young People's Congress in Hawaii in October 1999. A young man from Zimbabwe said in his address to the African caucus: "There needs to be more development projects led by the youth . . ." Youth-led development was not much featured as a phrase at that Congress: the young delegates were captivated by Gandhi's instruction to "be the change you want to see in the world". A young American even wrote a song entitled 'Be the Change!', and that phrase became the title of the Congress Report. Youth-led Development captures the essence of Gandhi's intention in his instruction. Basically he is telling citizens young and old: "Be the change! Don't wait around for others or governments to make changes you need in your life, your community, your country or your world. Make those changes yourself!"

In recent years, there has been a lot of talk in the development community about the 'rights-based approach' to childhood development. Since the arrival of the Convention on the Rights of the Child in the 1990s, children's organisations have campaigned for the all-but-two governments (USA and Somalia) who have signed the CRC to live up to their commitments and give children their rights. Alongside this, our Gandhian 'Be the Change' approach has been called, by the development community, the 'asset-based approach'. The two approaches are umbilically linked: for unless a child's rights to education, food, shelter, healthcare etc. are observed and protected, that child will not grow up to become the 'asset' that s/he should become for society.

There being no Convention on the Rights of Youth, YLD takes a proactive approach to the role of youth in development: 'Be the Change!' speaks up for the kind of self-reliance that successful, get-up-and-go / can-do societies everywhere have been built upon. It also combats the culture of entitlement and dependency which Nelson Mandela[11] and several American commentators[12] have spoken out against. In making the difficult transition from the world of school and parental care to autonomous living, many young people need a sharp kick to empower them to get out of the family home and earn their own living. The 'Be the Change!' YLD approach gives them the opportunity to pull themselves up by their bootstraps – to start a business, to do a project, to prove to themselves and others that they can operate on their own, and make a constructive contribution to their own and others' lives. Youth, unlike children, need to be given responsibility and opportunities for self-advancement. This is why I argue that development agencies should not lump children and youth together in the same department. Self-evidently, their needs are different: children require care, protection and assiduous recognition and provision of their rights as children; young people need support, autonomy, the provision of opportunities, responsibilities, training in marketable skills and empowerment as they emerge to become fully fledged adults in society.

Back in Hawaii, a cursory audit of the young people attending the Congress revealed that there was a great deal of YLD happening already: they just weren't calling it that. One young Kenyan told us that there are more than 3,000 informal youth associations operating in Kenya alone. Across sub-Saharan Africa, there are huge numbers of youth groups – operating well below the radar of government or the international donor community – doing health awareness programmes, self-help literacy instruction and IT programmes, starting small chicken, goat and pig farms and horticulture operations – creating small businesses with bicycle taxis or mobile phones.[13] These are the young people whom investments in YLD can help. They have proven already that they have the initiative. They have the ideas. They know what the needs of the community are and that they have the skills to address them. Though some of them are undoubtedly fatalistic and depressed about their prospects for an improved future, some of them, at least, have the dynamism and chutzpah to strive for a better life.

Following the Hawaii Congress, we knew we could prove that $100 invested in a youth-volunteer project could deliver the same value as one run by a professional development agency costing ten times as much. A ten-fold multiplication in value? We were very confident that the development ministries and ODA agencies would be interested.

We were so wrong. We got one interview! This was between a representative of a leading UK Aid NGO and Jagan Devaraj, our Be the Change representative in Bangalore, South India. We were told that the amounts we were looking at were too small and insignificant for major Aid NGOs to be interested: "It takes us as much staff time to manage a grant of $1,000 as it does to manage one of $1,000,000. So why would we be interested in managing small grants like this for youth?"

It is interesting to look back over the file now: of the then 22 Development Assistance Committee member countries, 13 didn't respond at all; five acknowledged our letter promising to get back to us (they never did); two said that they didn't consider youth as a sector – rather as a cross-cutting theme; and two said that the UK was not eligible for their development funding. When we asked OECD to explore the issue with us, they pointed us to their study about attitudes to development, which had a sector on youth. No one remotely understood the revolution in development we were proposing. Most still don't. I am told again and again that no one in the big agencies is interested in Youth-led Development, but I sense this might be changing. The Germans, Danes and Norwegians have recently created policies on children and youth/young people.[14] They all use the same definitions of the terms, which are:

- Children = Citizens aged 0-18 (the CRC definition)

- Youth = Citizens aged 15-24 (the United Nations definition)

- Young People = Citizens aged 0-25 (a generic term not officially defined)

UN-HABITAT, UNIDO and UNFPA now carry a torch for youth in development. UNICEF, UNDP and the World Bank are dipping their toes in the water. The big youth agencies are feeling bullish! It is a time of forward movement. A time for hope!

Back in 1999, we had no alternative but to set about administering YLD on our own. Working with young people themselves, we figured out a simple, cost-effective administration / management system for young people living at disadvantage – that would support them successfully to complete their Youth-led Social Enterprises (YLSEs) and their Youth-led Business Start-ups (YLBSUs). From day one we realised it had to be web-based, and that bridging the digital divide in terms of reporting and project submission had to be one of the priorities. We were fortunate to be able to develop the programme with NETAID, the UNDP Internet development portal, and Levi Strauss, who helped us build our first Be the Change! Youth-led Development website. We are also extremely fortunate to have partnered closely with Taking IT Global – the world's biggest youth activist web portal, with over 140,000 active young members. Building coalitions in this way, we were able to attract over 2,000 project proposals from young activists seeking to improve their communities through Youth-led Development. The breakdown of topic headings under which the YLD proposals fall is instructive: it shows where young people, right now, think they can make a contribution.[15]

TOPIC	TOTAL	%
Education & Skills Development	564	27
HIV-AIDS awareness	320	16
Income-Generating, YLBS-Us	282	14
IT, Media, Arts & Communication	272	13
Environment Conservation	176	9
Agriculture	126	6
Human Rights & Gender Issues	124	6
Youth facilities & organizations	72	3
Water	68	3
Miscellaneous	72	3
TOTALS	2,076	100

Youth and money

Ask any young African "What is your biggest obstacle to development?", and access to money always comes at the top of the list. It is at the front of their minds – and though development professionals can rationalise the absence of life-skills, training, project management skills etc. as the real obstacle, their perception will always put absence of capital at the top of their list. Absence of financial services has proved a huge obstacle in our own, humble YLD experiments. A young team want to install a pump in a distant rural village: how do you transfer the funds to them so that they can buy the pump, the cement, the sand and other materials to enable them to install it? We usually end up, as most of them do, buying the pump and the materials ourselves and delivering them – so that none of the young people ever actually see the money. However, cutting the young people off from handling their money is profoundly disempowering, and guarantees that they will never acquire the financial literacy to successfully run a small business. Historically, banks have always been at the root of development. This is why an early focus of any Nationwide YLD programme must be to set up a network of 'Barefoot Banks', transferring funds via mobile phones or other electronic means. Just as mobile phone technologies have leap-frogged the old technologies of copper wires, so the new financial infrastructures in the LDCs can be built using electronics, rather than building expensive real estate with safes, banknotes and ATMs. Young people can be in the forefront of creating this infrastructure, if they are given the opportunity. But so few are even acquainted with money, and they need the technical assistance and training to alert them to the opportunities for growth, self and community advancement that lie in the development of financial services within their countries.

Even where banks and infrastructure do exist, transferring funds and accounting for their use has always been challenging in LDCs. This is where the transparency of electronic transfers becomes useful – not just for the youth on the ground, but also for the aid donor. Equipped with bank cards and after being trained in the transfer of funds using pin codes, they can be the first in their community to learn about the uses of money – the different loan arrangements and reporting requirements they need to be successful. Soon Paypal and other internet transfer facilities will be available in all developing countries, and we can all move beyond the expensive, slow and desperately unreliable bank transfer system. Investing in YLD will ensure that young people are in the vanguard of this move to internet banking in the developing world – and in creating and advancing these moves lies one of the most tantalising opportunities that face the development community. It is one area where the presence of young, international volunteers will support the construction of solid, reliable financial services that can boost growth and help train young people who have never had experience in handling money to gain the financial literacy they need to run a small business or social enterprise.

Not that the local young people will need much help: our experience in getting money to the 200+ projects we have supported in extremely disadvantaged areas, via antediluvian bank transfer systems and corner shops in South London, prove this. To me, it's amazing that any of the projects have worked at all: that we have a 90+ percent completion rate is a vindication of the honesty, skill and resourcefulness of such young people.

Youth can do! – my own experience

In seeking to champion youth and the contribution they can make to development, it may help the reader to understand why, after 25 years, I retain incredible confidence in the capacity of young people to deliver. In doing so, I am well aware that some young people can be as venal, petty, mean and contemptible as any other sector of society: however, my conviction is that properly trained, motivated, mentored and guided any young person – yes ANY young person – can be transformed into a useful, productive member of society. That is the conviction that Prince Charles held when he started the Prince's Trust. He said:[16]

> "I feel very strongly that it is important to 'turn poachers into game-keepers'. One should not worry about the past records of such people. Occasionally things will go wrong. Occasionally some one runs off with the money. But they won't all do that. Having taken the risks, you find that we will get enormously beneficial results."

I agree! My 25 years' experience provides ample evidence that the vast majority of youth-led initiatives deliver amazingly beneficial results! Peace Child International – which I co-founded and run with my wife, Rosey, draws its name from a legend in Papua New Guinea (PNG), which goes like this:

> "When tribes of head-hunters make peace after a war, and it is a peace they mean to keep, they exchange two new born babies – one from each side. Each child grows up with the other's tribe and if, in the future, conflict threatens, the tribes send out these two children to negotiate the peace. Such a child is called a Peace Child." [17]

This story turned up in a BBC broadcast by Gerald Priestland on the night of our first *Peace Child* show at London's Royal Albert Hall in 1981. Ever since, it has provided the rationale for our Mission Statement: "Empowering young people." The PNG tribes empowered their young people to be peacemakers. So does *Peace Child*. They may, like us, have encountered what we call "Peace Monsters" – young people so headstrong, so confident of their ability, that they need no support. They are the exceptions. They must also have encountered young people consumed with nerves – sure that they cannot fulfil the expectations laid on them. So, like us, they would have had training programmes – with mentors and empowerers. Like us, they would expect the young people to deliver, and support them to do so. The feeling of adult support as a backstop for them if they falter – that is the purpose of any organisation working for Youth-led Development, and indeed, all education. Properly guided, empowered and supported to be successful, all young people can succeed – succeed beyond their wildest dreams and those of their parents, friends and teachers. Successful Youth-led Development needs that support infrastructure to be in place before any large-scale investments are made.

But they need to be flexible. Thus support was in place for the first production of the *Peace Child* musical: I had written a good script – good lines for a variety of different children; compelling narrative, good jokes! It was all in place. But driving the children of the cast home from rehearsals, I found their conversations in the back of the car about the nuclear issue – and their jokes were better and funnier than those I had given them in the script. So I would go back at night and re-write some of the dialogue to include their ideas, and give them new pages of script at the next rehearsal. Sometimes they would notice their ideas and I would own up to the theft! Mostly they were thrilled as they felt that they themselves were becoming the Peace Children of the story. As one child said: "To stand on stage and say lines that you have written yourself to an audience of your parents and friends, that's awesome!" And it was – and all over the USA, the USSR and several other countries, *Peace Child* gave the children that opportunity. I believe I am one of very few playwrights whose first instruction to his cast is: "Tear up my play and start again . . ." I ask them to do this because I know that most of the time, what the children come up with will be more interesting – and certainly more authentic to them – than anything I can write for them. And in giving them that ownership of the play, I was also giving them the chance to experience their own power – their own creativity and talent.

Years later, I waited in Moscow for the first American students to arrive to do the premiere of the first Soviet-American performance of *Peace Child*. I should explain that the *Peace Child* story tells of a young Russian girl who befriends a young American boy at an embassy cocktail party. Together, through many adventures, they persuade their presidents to become friends and work for peace as they have done – and not for a nuclear war that would destroy the world. So doing the play with Russian and American young people was a breakthrough I had worked towards for several years. The Minister of Culture had regularly refused to even discuss allowing Soviet children to take part in what he termed a "decadent Western Rock Musical". However, with the new winds of Gorbachev's *glasnost* and *perestroika* blowing through the corridors of Soviet bureaucracy, he had agreed to watch a performance of *Peace*

Child and consider granting the Russians exit visas to enable the Soviet cast to travel to the USA to perform the play across North America.

Over a million dollars had been raised in the USA to welcome them and promote the performances in 12 cities. A great deal, therefore, was riding on the success of this audition performance but, as always, we were determined to stay true to the 'process' and support the young people to write the play themselves. So when the Americans' flight was delayed – first one – then two – and ultimately three days – I became intensely worried. They arrived on the Sunday night – dog-tired, jet-lagged – some of them quite sick. They were all aware that the crucial audition performance was on the Thursday afternoon – giving us just three and a half days to write, rehearse, choreograph and learn the lines and songs of a two-act musical – to be done mostly in Russian for the Minister of Culture spoke no word of English. Impossible! Out of the question, my head told me.

But on the Monday morning, the American and Russian cast gathered for their first meeting and, without hesitation, agreed to go for it! And they did! By the Thursday, the young people put on a pretty respectable performance of a new script, written by themselves using the *Peace Child* framework with songs and dances that did credit to all of them. And the Minister was moved to tears. At the end this big bear of a man who had represented the barrier between us and a world-beating North American tour had dissolved. He joined the cast on stage, putting his big arms around them, and telling them about his children. He loved them – and he gave the visas for an exercise that would bring the first Soviet kids to the USA on a Youth Exchange in 1986, punching a big hole through the Iron Curtain through which thousands of young Russians and young Americans would follow in the ensuing years – many of them on Peace Child exchanges.

And it was entirely due to the courage, ability, and superhuman energy of those 30 kids who came together in a Moscow conference centre that Monday morning. Supported, it has to be said, by adult musicians, choreographers and directors who were not about to give up either. But we were all amazed by the commitment of the young people. They delivered. As indeed they have continued to deliver for me and Peace Child International down the years.

A decade letter, we had a commission from the United Nations to produce a children's edition of Agenda 21 – a 96-page full colour illustrated book distilling the key messages of the 800-page Rio Earth Summit Agenda 21 and linking them to young people's own lived experience. The budget was not generous, and only allowed 21 days for the 'Editorial Meeting' that would produce the finished book ready for the printers. Too late we heard the advice of publishers: "Impossible! You would need at least three months even for professionals. Kids? – you're talking six to 10 months!" We had no alternative but to go for it. We collected paintings, stories, poems and opinion pieces from children around the world. Then 21 of the best young authors and illustrators from 16 countries met at a youth centre in rural England. They struggled – several of the best artists did not speak a word of English! But they got a sense of the urgency, and for 20 days (and often nights) they worked – cutting and pasting the book together (this was before the days of desktop publishing). One Turkish girl worked 72 hours straight – so anxious was she to have 'her' pages perfect. And in the end, it was ready! And the kids celebrated with free passes to a U2 concert at Wembley Stadium. The publishers spent a few days tidying it up – correcting typos etc. – but the book was essentially as the kids delivered it. And it went on to sell over half a million copies, and to be translated into 23 languages.

I tell these stories, not to show off, but rather to explain my conviction, articulated by my friend, Andrew Simmonds of the Commonwealth Youth Programme, that "young people, properly trained and supported, can rise to pretty much any challenge that you throw at them." I have spent my adult life devolving insane amounts of responsibility on to their young shoulders – and very, very rarely have they let me down. Young people deliver! And I believe they can deliver on their promise to make poverty history – which is why ODA agencies should support them.

Three Slogans

ONE: *Habitat TWO – Youth Can Do!*

"Habitat TWO – Youth Can Do!" was the slogan of the Youth Caucus at the Istanbul Habitat Conference in 1995. UN-HABITAT is one of the few UN agencies that has maintained an intelligent commitment to youth programming over the years. They realise – and have ample proof – that Youth Can Do! They are also the first UN agency to use the phrase Youth-led Development. They define it as follows:[18]

• The development of youth capacity to undertake social, environmental and economic enterprise for the benefit of their community;

- In place of the traditional teacher-student model, YLD cultivates in youth multiple capacities – the skills, attitudes and discipline to be self-reliant, self-motivated and self-organised;

- YLD is best facilitated through engagement with adults and peer leaders, who will actively seek and promote opportunities for them to gain real world leadership and vocational skills.

They argue that the rationale behind YLD is its multiplier effect: youth respect peer leadership, and are apt to listen and follow their example. By developing young leaders, we are essentially building allies who can greatly multiply local, national and international development efforts.

However, UN-HABITAT recognises the widespread implementation of YLD strategies requires a fundamental paradigm shift. Youth must no longer be seen as problems requiring expenditure of resources, but rather they should be considered as investment opportunities: assets for development. Youth-led Development recognises that youth have a stake in the same development issues that affect other segments of the population. It places young people (future leaders) in the mainstream of decision-making on these issues.

In April 2007, the UN-Habitat Governing Council agreed to establish a Youth Fund[19] to ensure the sustainability and expansion of the agency's efforts in youth-led development. The fund will support youth-led initiatives in the following areas:

- Mobilising young people to help strengthen youth-related policy formulation;

- Building capacities of governments, civil society organisations and the private sector to better address youth needs and issues

- Supporting the development of best practice information and communication-oriented networks;

- Piloting innovative approaches to employment, good governance, adequate shelter and secure tenure

- Facilitating vocational training and credit mechanisms to promote entrepreneurship and employment for young women and men, in collaboration with private sector and other UN bodies

- Promoting gender mainstreaming in all activities of urban youth.

UN-Habitat Executive Director, Mrs Anna Tibaijuka, explained:

"The Youth Fund reflects our growing commitment to address the problems of urban youth. Young people, lest we forget, constitute the majority of the urban population in rapidly urbanising countries. Often, they have no jobs and no voice. Any effective response to improving the living conditions of the urban poor and slum dwellers must deal, prima facie, with the challenges facing youth." [20]

The establishment of the Youth Fund was called for at the Youth Assembly of the World Urban Forum (Vancouver, June 2006). Some 500 youth delegates representing hundreds of youth-led organisations recommended it as part of the Youth Engagement Strategy.[21] The government of Norway sponsored the proposal to establish the youth fund. Erik Berg of Norway's Ministry of Foreign Affairs stated:

"There is an urgent need to begin a process of mainstreaming youth in development strategies, particularly in the context of sustainable urban development, and we believe the UN-Habitat should be a lead agency in this process, and we further believe that establishment of a dedicated fund for targeted support of youth-led initiatives can be an excellent mechanism for implementing this." [22]

Habitat goes on to state:

"The Youth Fund will represent a notable milestone marking recognition at the highest levels of the need to support, practically, youth-led initiatives, and lead the way for other organisations and governments to place youth at the centre of their development strategies. The UN-HABITAT website (www.unhabitat.org) lists 38 supporting organisations. Many more have offered their endorsements. UN-HABITAT has always been extremely supportive of youth involvement in their programmes – from the Habitat TWO initiative at the Istanbul Summit, through their consistent support for Youth at the World Youth Festivals, the Hip-Hop initiative etc."

Thank you UN-HABITAT! Your Youth Fund is perhaps the finest implementation by any agency of the stated request of this Briefing, "to place youth at the centre of their development strategies".

TWO: *See youth as a resource, not a problem*

At another UN Conference in Johannesburg, seven years after Istanbul, the youth caucus adopted an even more resonant slogan that guides every syllable of this Briefing: "See youth as a resource, not a problem." Daily, throughout the world, many millions of young people are just that. A powerful economic and social resource, they are forced to care for their siblings, care for disabled or sick parents, put food on the table for them, run businesses, tend to animals. In the UK alone, a recent study found that 175,000 children are caring for sick, disabled or incapable parents.[23] We hear this, and we are sickened for, in some way, these children are being robbed of their childhood. This is tragic. But instead of barging in and taking over, a caring society should allow the young people themselves to dictate how they want to adjust and improve their lives. For vulnerable young people, Youth-led Development is even more of an imperative than for the non-vulnerable ones.

The slogan often leads to the interesting debate on where Youth-led Development ends and child labour begins. A tricky one, this, as getting youth to volunteer for community development tasks can very easily be perceived to be exploitation of youthful goodwill. Unions and professional interest groups can rightly get concerned that young people are being asked to do for free what their members seek good wages for doing. This is why in this paper I stress that Youth-led Development is essentially education: the best kind of experiential education, which delivers community benefits as well as major benefits to the young person doing it. Young people do not get paid to go to school. Why complain therefore when they are invited to participate in YLD projects that provide a better kind of education and actually produce some visible benefit to themselves and to their communities? The essential difference between YLD and child labour is that YLD is voluntary: the young people do it because they want to, not because some adult orders them to. There is no compulsion.

YLD respects young people as an asset, an amazing asset to society. Some young people fall short of our expectations, as do many adults. But we must have the highest aspirations for our young people: we must combat the media in which 80 percent of articles and programmes about youth present them in a negative light. Such presentational attitudes deliver self-fulfilling prophecies. We need to become positive and respectful in our attitude towards young people. We must lay out their generational challenge: 'to make poverty history in a sustainable way in their lifetimes' – in the confident belief that they can do it. That confidence must be transmitted in every word of every policy document – every utterance of every politician and commentator, every lesson of every teacher and professor and, vitally, every word of every parent! Only by burying the negative perceptions of youth in a storm of positive impressions – the music, the art, the creativity, energy, talent, brilliance and skills of youth – will young people themselves begin to live the self-fulfilling prophecy that they are, as Kofi Annan points out,"the most precious resource our planet possesses".

THREE: *Give Young People a chance to Make Poverty History!*

"Give young people a chance to make poverty history" was our slogan for the 2005 Make Poverty History campaign. It didn't get much ink in the media, but my conviction remains that they deserve – and require – to be given that chance. And that their whole education, from the day they enter primary school to the day they graduate from their university, should be centrally focussed on equipping them to make the most of that chance when they get it. For we live in a time when we not only have ample capacity to make poverty history if we want to; we also live in a time when – if the eco-pessimists like James Lovelock are right – humanity faces environmental asphyxiation and a steep decline in population. Even if Lovelock is wrong, every politician is now aware that the challenge of achieving sustainable lifestyles is a priority for human security. Ending poverty in a sustainable way is thus the main challenge that school – whether formal or informal – should be equipping young people for. But it isn't. Educators and educational authorities have blithely ignored the Agenda 21 instruction to "re-orientate education towards sustainability".[24] In 2005, UNESCO launched the Decade of Education for Sustainability, designed to help educators re-order their priorities to the science and economics of sustainability. However, government support for the Decade is timid, and few educators have been equipped with the necessary skills.

Schumacher himself would have approved of the goals of the Decade – sustainability is at the heart of Buddhist economics. 'Enoughness' should be the guiding ethos of all that is taught in schools, and young people intuitively know this. They relate closely to animals and the environment. That care can be translated into their business and social enterprises, with a little support and guidance. YLD can thus help produce that sea change in attitude so necessary in education. Instead of timid moves towards 'youth participation,' we call for massive investment in youth-adult co-management so that young people can become equal partners with their elders, centrally involved in the decisions that will set humanity on a well-planned course to ensure our survival as a species.

Right now, young people are not given that chance called for in this slogan. They continue to be seen as a problem to be contained and managed rather

Seven toilets for the 1,000 residents of the Mandela Camp for internally displaced people.

The new toilets which brought a whole new atmosphere of hope to the refugees – and great respect for James and his team.

James Koruma's street with sewage flowing down the middle of it.

James Koruma pumps clean water from the newly installed pump with the water supply and sewage in separate plastic pipes.

Bee-keeping in India — a great way for young people to earn money and create a nutritious food supplement for themselves and their families.

A French volunteer teaches the mysteries of IT to eager young students in Ecuador.

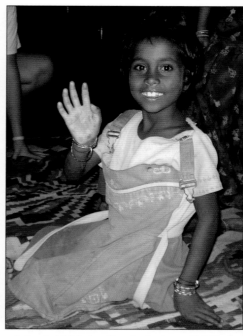

A street child finds refuge in the Peace Child India creche, allowing her mother to go out to work.

The logo of a Kibera slum project in Nairobi, Kenya, to teach unmarried mothers to bake and sell delicious cookies.

Harbou Village Fish Pond, Cambodia – dug by students and staff to attract students from poor backgrounds back to school by offering them free fish lunches.

Alpha Bacar Barry (far right) and members of the youth network who prepared the MRU-YEF Proposal.

Peace Child's World Youth Congress — a celebration of Youth-led Development.
Delegates applaud success at the 3rd Congress in Stirling, Scotland, August 2005.

James Wolfensohn, former President of the World Bank, is honoured with the Champion of Youth Award, World Youth Congress 2005.

The 'Be the Change' logo, inspired by Mahatma Ghandi's line: "You have to be the change you want to see in the world!"

than a resource to be supported and employed. In the corridors of government and large institutions, there is no understanding of, or enthusiasm for, the fact that 'Youth Can Do!' And so youth linger on the margins of society – citizens-in-waiting in a shadow land of missed opportunities and challenges only vaguely defined and barely articulated in the formal, assessed part of the curriculum. Our best chance for saving the planet slips through our fingers, day by day, week by week, year by year as yet more waves of young people arrive on the beach of adulthood, unaware of their power to make a difference.

"In this new century, millions of people in the world's poorest countries remain imprisoned, enslaved – trapped in the prison of poverty.

It is time to set them free. Like slavery and apartheid, poverty is not natural. It is man-made and it can be overcome and eradicated by the actions of human beings. And overcoming poverty is not a gesture of charity. It is an act of justice. It is the protection of a fundamental human right, the right to dignity and a decent life. While poverty persists, there is no true freedom.

This white band is from my country. Today, I want to give this band to you, young people of Britain. I entrust it to you. I will be watching you with anticipation. Sometimes it falls upon a generation to be great. You can be that great generation. Let your greatness blossom. Make Poverty History. Then we can all stand with our heads held high." – **Nelson Mandela, launching the Make Poverty History Campaign, London 2005**

Chapter Two

Youth-led Development:
an Irresistible Proposition

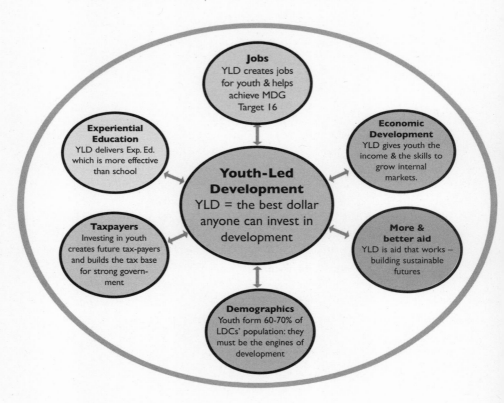

The graphic above summarises the six main reasons that make YLD an irresistible proposition. However, at the risk of offending every young person in my YLD network, let me start by outlining a seventh: cost-effectiveness.

In the Executive Summary I mentioned the figure of $430,000[1] that the USAID website gives as the cost of putting one US expatriate into the field in a developing country. In my search to find out how they arrive at that figure, I have found development agencies, particularly USAID, to be extremely secretive. However, a few well-placed threats of invoking the Freedom of Information Act, and discussions with friends who have worked in aid agencies overseas, reveal that such figures, far from being unusual, are fairly standard for most expatriate development professionals working overseas.

The results of a very informal 'Don't Quote Me' investigation reveals the cost breakdown as follows:

Salary	120,000
Health insurance	20,000
Housing allowance	37,000
Moving allowance	30,000
Hardship benefits	35,000
Air-conditioned, 4WD SUV	48,000
Driver	15,000
House-keeping staff allowance	20,000
Share of office overhead costs	90,000
Secretary (local staff)	15,000
TOTAL	$430,000

Compare this to the costs associated with assigning a young volunteer from Europe, Asia, North or Latin America alongside a local volunteer – the "pairing approach" that is now favoured by almost every major international volunteer agency. In other words, we are comparing the price of TWO well-educated, skilful, committed young people each engaged in practical development projects, but also engaged together on a learning journey designed to develop the policies that will wipe poverty off the face of the planet in a sustainable way.

Cost of installing one international and one local YLD volunteer in an African village with Project Fund:

Daily food allowance x 2 @ $2.50 ea. x 365	1,825
Annual centre rental – hostel & office	1,250
Weekly pocket money x 2 @ $20 pw x 52	2,080
Petrol & depreciation on 1 x 250cc motor-cycle per year:	800
Depreciation on furnishings & computers	1,000
Cost to recruit, train and orientate of 2 volunteers:	5,695
Flights for volunteer (from London)	1,000
Full medical/repatriation insurance	350
Project Fund	10,000
Sub-total	**24,000**

Sub-total brought forward	**24,000**
Salary	0
Moving allowance	0
Hardship benefits	0
Car	0
Driver	0
Housekeeping staff allowance	0
Air-conditioned office	0
Secretary (local staff)	0
TOTAL	**$ 24,000**

So there could be 18 trained YLD professionals, with a $10,000 project fund for each pair of them, for the price of one government, NGO or UN Agency professional. This is why we are confident that, when YLD goes to scale, we can prove that young people can deliver 10 to 20 times more value per dollar than development professionals.

To me, the economic arguments represent the heart of the irresistible proposition that is YLD. In a world where development dollars are at a premium, it surely makes sense to stretch each one as far as possible. Because this call for YLD funding takes place in the context of rising ODA budgets, we are not threatening to replace the PhD professionals: YLD volunteers need their professional support as an essential component of their mentoring systems. Local and overseas professionals with years of experience of dealing with the economic, social and planning challenges of development need to be woven into the fabric of YLD policy – not as leaders or gatekeepers, but as equal partners. And, crucially, YLD needs local and national government partnership, sharing their priorities, and identifying those areas where government feels youth can be most helpful.

But young people deeply resent the inclusion of this item as evidence of the value of YLD. It lowers them to the level of 'development on the cheap!'[2] which is the last thing I want to suggest. Because of the six other benefits I am going to outline, I would argue that, even if YLD were more expensive than elder-led development, it would be a fantastically worthwhile investment. Let's explore in turn each of the six benefits listed on the flower logo:

1. Demographics Young people under 25 form 51 percent of the world's population,[3] the biggest cohort of young people the world has ever seen. In the poorest countries the percentages are even larger: 60-70 percent.

Logic should dictate that governments put this majority sector of the population at the heart of their development policy. As beneficiaries of development aid, in terms of training, healthcare, primary education, food and social welfare, their chances in life can be improved immeasurably by becoming a focus area for donor investment. By embracing the concept of youth-led development, this vast sector of the population becomes an incredible asset and partner for government in the field of aid delivery. They should be the first choice for delivery of peer-to-peer teaching programmes, HIV-AIDS awareness programmes,[4] private sector growth through youth-led business start-ups etc. This is the majority sector of the population! What more compelling reason does one need to put the focus upon them?

2. Experiential Education In a recent lecture[5] David Orr, the celebrated American environmental educator, set out the following startling statistics about the extent to which information conveyed in different media in schools is retained by students:

Medium	Retention Rate
Cognitive – *front of the class, formal classroom instruction*	15%
Reading a book	30%
Experiential Education – *learning by doing a task related to the information*	75%
Peer-to-Peer Teaching – *youth-teaching-youth on the information*	90%

The evidence of the effectiveness of experiential education has been proven time and time again in study after study. Likewise, the power of Peer-to-Peer teaching: not only is it a cost-effective programme for communicating basic skills as the Child-to-Child and Each-one-Teach-one reading programmes have proved – Orr's research proves the value to the peer teacher. Anyone who has ever taught IT in a school knows this to be the case: students teach each other and thereby consolidate and reinforce their own knowledge and skills.

Life is so hard for young people from disadvantaged backgrounds in the poorest countries that the idea of voluntarism – working for free – is not attractive or even possible for most of them. However, remember: YLD is at heart an educational experience: they, or their parents, pay for them to go to school. Why should they not volunteer for an education that is self-evidently more effective than school, especially as they get their food, housing and pocket money and the amazing benefit of working alongside a young volunteer from another country who can expand their world vision – and their sense of their own potential – in the space of a few weeks. "Experience the thrill of unity!" was a watchword in our early *Peace Child* performances. And it is a thrill – the different languages, different cultures, different life stories – all are objects of fascination for young minds. They grow immensely in the international context. And, rubbing shoulders with Europeans, Africans, Asians and Americans who have the benefit of expensive education, feeds their minds with skills, talents and awareness in everything from IT to financial literacy to global politics. It gives young people living at a disadvantage the sensation that they might really be able to make something of their lives. Our YLD programme provides them with the support and mentorship that reinforces that self-belief every day. The increase in their competencies (IT and project management skills mainly) and self confidence is worth a vast price in any development equation.

For the international volunteer, whether from Europe, Asia, North America or a Southern neighbour, the benefits are equally life-changing, as any VSO or Peace Corps graduate will confirm.

3. Youth Job Creation In survey after survey[6] of our young people's networks in poor countries, the answer comes back that young people's top priority is "getting a good job!" In West Africa we, in Peace Child, have been focussing upon the challenge of finding such jobs, which can be laid out as follows:[7]

Country Name	Total Population	% Youth Population Under 25	% Youth Unemployed	Total Youth Unemployed
Cote D'Ivoire	18,200,000	67.1%	31%	3,658,292
Guinea	9,400,000	63.6%	58%*	3,588,312
Liberia	3,300,000	64.5%	88%	1,806,288
Sierra Leone	5,300,000	62.2%	60%	2,051,100

That's 11 million young people looking for jobs in just four relatively small countries. The International Labour Organisation tells us there are 88 million youth unemployed, and that youth unemployment in LDCs is double or triple the general rate.[8] There are 1.2 billion young people aged 15-24 in the world today, and the next generation will be 1.8 billion.[9] More than 200 million youth live in poverty, 130 million are illiterate and 10 million are living with HIV/AIDS. There are 125 million working youth living in a household where there is less than US$1 a day available per head, and 300 million where there's less than US$2 per head.[10] Is it any wonder that the cry of young people for what the ILO calls "Decent Work" is noisy and vociferous? Rick Little, of the ImagineNations Group, puts it like this:

> "Over the next decade, more than one billion young people will enter the global labor market. Experts predict, optimistically, that no more than 300 million new jobs will be created during this same period. Furthermore, an average 72 percent of young people in developing countries are not in school past age 14. If they are not in school and there are no jobs in the formal economy, what are their options? Developing innovative new partnerships that provide young adults with access to financial services and products, including business coaching, savings, investments and loans will be absolutely essential to securing a more peaceful, prosperous and hopeful future."

YLD provides several solutions to the youth unemployment crisis: Youth-led Business Start-ups (YLBS-Us), Youth-led Social Enterprises (YLSEs – health care, peer-to-peer teaching, elderly care etc.) and Youth-led Labour Intensive Infrastructure Projects (YLLIIPs) are all accepted by the major aid agencies to be amongst the most promising strategies for youth job creation. The youth themselves and local elders also agree.

This is perhaps the best reason for investing heavily in YLD. There are also strong social grounds for making such investments: unemployed youth turn to crime, fall prey to drugs, prostitution, anti-social behaviour and – worst – to rebel groups who offer them food, friends and shelter plus the excitement of revolution. In extreme cases, they turn to 'suicide job-seeking' – climbing aboard leaky boats to sail to the Canaries, knowing that only about half of them will make it. Solving the youth unemployment problem is the only Millennium Development Goal that mentions youth (Target 16, Goal 8). But jobs will not be created by writing reports or the ILO wishing it were so: a programme of sustained, intelligent investment in YLD is the best way to secure the creation of jobs on the ground. All stakeholders should collaborate with youth to achieve them.

4. Sustainable Economic Development Once the jobs and the energy are generated in and by the young generation, economic growth is the inevitable consequence. The impact of several tens of thousands of peer-educated IT experts with the experience of starting and managing small social or commercial enterprises will be immediate and beneficial. And the young people will be excellent partners in the drive to improve the regulatory environment. They have no sense of the impossible! With a nation-wide YLD programme in place (with the support of international volunteers who would be aghast at the mediaeval and often ridiculously corrupt regulatory systems in place in developing countries), young leaders will quickly come together and design alternatives and, with their critical mass, put pressure on authorities to ensure that regulatory changes are made. Reformers will find an invaluable ally in YLD. Likewise, if young people are alerted to the challenges awaiting them in the post-fossil fuel world, YLD will provide powerful support to those seeking low-carbon paths to energy provision.

Sustainable economic development could also be accelerated if the international volunteers learn and experience first-hand the appalling unfairness of the current trade/subsidy regime. When they see that access to western markets is obstructed, not just by antiquated regulatory regimes in the developing world, but also by their own western governments' $352 billion trade subsidy payments,[11] they will be compelled to join the grassroots movements campaigning for change. Such change would be the single biggest boost to economic growth – and making poverty history – in the world's least developed countries. YLD will raise the campaign for change in the global trade/subsidy regime more powerfully than any other economic strategy.

5. Expanding the Tax Base The Canadian branch of Youth Business International recently sought a new grant of C$10 million from the government of Canada to expand their programme of youth business start-up loans. Part of the argument for the new loan was that the previous C$10 million in grant aid had started up companies which, together, had paid the government C$30 million in taxes. The government was persuaded. They got their grant.[12]

Developing countries are obviously in a different position, but they are becoming more self-reliant. Aid flows as a percentage of GDP are moving in the right direction, down from 12 percent in 1990 to just under 10 percent in 2004.[13] But several countries, such as Sierra Leone, receive a third of their GDP in foreign aid and loans.[14] This means that, currently, the salaries of most politicians and government officials are paid by international aid donors. Their Mercedes cars, personal security teams, luxury ministerial villas and lavish government expense accounts are paid for by western tax-payers. That is a huge democratic deficit for these countries. It separates them entirely from responsibility to their own people and puts them in the pay of western donor agencies.The goal of the IFF and all other efforts to 'front-load'[15] overseas development assistance is to end the dependency of LDC governments on western aid, and generate an indigenous tax base to support and pay for government activities. However, all too often aid dependency has led to laziness in government and inefficient tax collection regimes which frequently 'forget' to collect tax from government employ-ees and politicians, and which often grant export licences for minerals and other goods that sell the country's birthright for a song.

Young people in these countries are not inclined to learn about, or pay, taxes to what they perceive to be a corrupt and inefficient government. However, this is a self-defeating downward spiral. Until they get a wider tax base, governments in developing countries cannot improve their services or tackle corruption. The result is increasing disconnect between people and government, and a widening democratic deficit as governments pay more attention to the concerns of their western paymasters than they do to their own citizens who are too poor, or plain unwilling, to pay them any tax.

YLD aims to change this by making registration a condition of invest-ment in YLBS-Us: inevitably, these small, youth-run businesses will not have the revenue to pay much in the way of taxes in the early years, but if, in the minds of the young managers, there is an understanding and a habit built up to pay tax and contribute to strong, transparent, corruption-free government, a feeling of ownership of that government will begin to emerge, which is not there at all at the moment. Slowly, governments will have to become accountable to their own people, to their own private sec-tor. An increasingly prosperous private sector will demand better perfor-mance from government in the regulatory field, and in the services they provide to train and educate the young population.

Ending the dependency of governments on Western aid is the long-term goal of all Western donors: by training, supporting and investing in the youth of today, Western donors can help to ensure that by the time these young people become the government leaders of tomorrow, they will be supported by domestic tax revenue, not handouts from overseas.

6. More and Better Aid Roger Riddell, in his recent book *Does Foreign Aid really Work?*, writes:

> "Aid has made a difference, but it could make a far greater difference. Lives have been saved, livelihoods improved and poverty reduced but much more could have been done. The Samaritan's Dilemma is that the more aid we give, the less effort the recipients exert to improve themselves."

Robert Cassen, author of the earlier study, *Does Aid Work?* said at the launch of Riddell's book that he had visited Tanzania in 2007 and could not see what development aid had achieved there. He said: "$500 million dollars worth of aid has been delivered there over the last three decades, and I couldn't see a trace of it." P. J. O'Rourke had exactly the same reaction.[17] Statistically, over the past decades, the march of human progress has, in many poorer countries, become a retreat. The call for "more and better aid", which was a central plank of the 2005 Make Poverty History Campaign, recognises this. It is an opinion shared by most donors. In March 2005, donor and recipient (or 'partner') country ministers met in Paris to agree a Declaration on Aid Effectiveness,[18] seeking to improve aid harmonisation, alignment, results, mutual accountability and give more ownership of the aid process to the partner country governments. It begins:

> "We, Ministers of developed and developing countries responsible for promoting development, resolve to take far-reaching and monitorable actions to reform the ways we deliver and manage aid. We recognise that while the volumes of aid and other development resources must increase to achieve these goals, aid effectiveness must increase significantly as well, to support partner country efforts to strengthen governance and improve development performance."

The acknowledgement that aid effectiveness must increase is the closest that government ministers and development professionals will ever come to admitting that current aid policies are NOT working. In the experience of many young people, it is self-evidently not working, and that is why we claim the right to try to test our hypothesis that "YLD is the best dollar you will ever invest in overseas development." Note the word 'invest' – we expect a measurable return on each YLD investment. We are anxious to test our YLD hypothesis in a variety of locations and situations, but especially we want to test it in the poorest countries. Our hypothesis is that such YLD investments, nationwide, will result in those countries leaping ahead after five years. The resilience, energy, creativity and skills of youth will, we believe, guarantee it.

Examples of their innovation and capacity to deliver more and better aid than comparable investments in the elder-led sector – are legion! My greatest delight in working with young people these last 27 years has been their incredible capacity to surprise me with their 'can-do' spirit and ability to innovate. I made a little film about one of them: Kaloka Alama lives in a small village above Freetown, the Sierra Leone capital, in a valley where all the trees had been felled for firewood during the civil war. In the rainy season, fertile earth was being washed away, with the valley becoming a desert before their eyes. Kaloka determined to re-plant the forest – 100,000 trees. He planted them all from seed, grew them in a nursery, then planted them out with his friends. It took him five years, but the forest now flourishes. Sanitation, likewise: we had a group who completely renovated an old colonial sewage works in a remote town in the Atlas Mountains of Morocco. Roads, the same: the South Africans have the Expanded Public Works Programme which has built over 1,000 km of roads with young people, training and motivating them to be effective workers at the same time.[19]

With the right encouragement, mentorship and financial support, young people just get on with the job. They need very little incentive to Be the Change!

Benefits to International Volunteers & Sending Countries

The US Peace Corps has three main political goals. To

1. Export American values – peace, tolerance, democracy and the rule of law;

2. Provide concrete, measurable assistance to disadvantaged peoples;

3. Bring benefits back to the USA with the returning volunteers.

Whenever Peace Corps leaders are called to Congress to argue for budget increases, they only ever mention the third goal.[20] For the evidence is irrefutable: the 500,000 returning Peace Corps volunteers have immensely enriched the United States, working as the voluntary school governors, town and village counsellors, public servants of all kinds. Search the staff lists of any of the great US charitable and service agencies, and you will find ex-Peace Corps volunteers in key positions. The Peace Corps experience engrains in them the value, the satisfaction and the sheer fun of service: the idea summed up in that great Kennedy line: "Ask not what your country can do for you – ask what you can do for your country",[21] though for this paper, we would ask Kennedy to replace the word "country" by "world".

One day, we shall try to put a figure on the value of the volunteer service provided to the USA by ex-Peace Corps volunteers. We guess the figure would be in the billions. Other countries – Canada, Norway, Germany, Austria, the UK, the Netherlands and others – have also experienced the rewards of returning volunteers generating a culture of service and volunteerism back home. The awakening that takes place, the understanding of the real priorities in life, the love and empathy for disadvantaged people and places in the world, is an invaluable societal benefit. Likewise, the development of practical skills of working in the globalised business arena delivers employability skills of great value to their future private sector employers. The young volunteers should, and in many cases do, pay for the experience of overseas voluntary service. For many young people, the experience is a superb supplement to, and practical application of, all that they have learned in school.

Many young people in our constituency have complained of the rip-off fees charged by some operators – thousands of pounds for a six-week experience that is rarely of much use to either the receiving organisation or the young volunteer.[21] Happily, the UK-based independent campaigning group Tourism Concern is issuing a code of conduct that will require companies to prove that the projects they send students to are long-term and sustainable, not just established hastily to meet the latest fashionable cause or popular destination. Companies that operate in this multi-million-pound 'voluntourism' market will be blacklisted if they do not comply. This is a good start – but there is a lot more work to be done: most receiving NGOs in developing countries need the sustained commitment of one to two years from each volunteer.

I trust it is clear that we are talking about a very different kind of experience and service provided by the YLD international volunteer. For a start, the requests will come first from our developing country partners, not from Western agencies seeking placements. The volunteers will be trained to respond to specific needs. And they will always work in pairs with local, indigenous volunteers – to whom they will report at all times.

They have to be the right young people, of course: selection is 9/10ths of a successful international volunteer programme. Mistakes are bound to happen, but because the experience of a bad volunteer is incredibly stressful and negative for the receiving community, it is imperative for policy makers and YLD professionals to keep these errors to a minimum by investing in very careful recruitment and training regimes. Also, the receiving community must reserve the right to send home any international volunteer who is not serving them satisfactorily. Local volunteers need training too, as city-based, elite kids often have worse attitudes to rural people than the international volunteers. Both have to be taught the basic technologies of how to support and empower young people living at great disadvantage in rural or urban communities to haul themselves out of poverty by their own creativity, skills and hard work.

Conclusion

Benefits, benefits, benefits! YLD is the ultimate win-win-win-win situation! When you add up all the benefits described here, it is impossible to think of any other development investment that delivers so many short and long-term benefits to the developing country community. I called my original essay on Youth-led Development, "Investing in Happiness" – for that is essentially what it is: it brings untold happiness to young people and their communities. The self-esteem and self-confidence of the young people rise visibly before your eyes as they realise they 'can do something!' Their attitudes towards the world, and often their academic performance, improve measurably. And, just as any parent rejoices and is absurdly proud when their baby takes its first step, so community elders are visibly inspired by their young citizens taking the time and the trouble to improve the communities in which they live. On their own. Without adult leadership.

Chapter Three
The Evidence of Success

"Promising but unproven..." The phrase echoes darkly through the World Bank's World Development Report on *Development and the Next Generation.*[1]

True – the disaggregated data on Youth-led Development does not exist: when did you last meet a professor of Youth-led Development at one of the big University Research Departments, or government think-tanks? They don't exist – and thus there can be no sound base of evidence on which to win the argument for the effectiveness of YLD.

Right?

Wrong! Because academic evidence is not the only evidence we need. If we had had to wait for academic evidence to support the argument for including the 50 percent of the world's population that is female in development policy, women would likely be still waiting. There is a ton of evidence to support the idea of investing in youth-led development. From the simple brilliance of composers like Mozart, poets like John Keats and gymnasts like Nadia Komenic, the world is full of young personalities who have made a massive mark on the world before their 25th birthdays. The modern IT industry was mostly built by people under 25 – from the Steves (Jobs and Wozniak) who created Apple computers in their garage, to Bill Gates dropping out from Harvard to start Microsoft, to the dotcom millionaires, many of whom made their millions in their teens.

Fine – but composing symphonies or founding software companies is not what young people need, or have the opportunity to do, in remote African villages. And most teenagers are not Mozart or Bill Gates: are there things that the average teenager can accomplish easily to improve their community? Answer is YES – thousands!

World Bank Evidence

The *World Development Report* is littered with the kind of evidence which I, for one, find extremely compelling. For example Chapter 7, "Exercising citizenship", opens with an inspiring story of 24 students from the University of Lahore who, following the Kashmir earthquake, volunteered to survey house damage: they surveyed 3,500 households covering 32,000 individuals, reporting back to donors, and targeting assistance where it was most urgently needed. There is no doubt that their work saved lives. The report is liberally sprinkled with other anecdotes of extraordinary youth contributions.

On its last page, the Report states: "This Report's simple message to governments and policy makers is that investing in young people is essential for development…" It adds: "For those investments to be most effective, young people must be included as stakeholders in decisions that affect them." It goes on to list tips and examples of how young people can help more in the development process – in a way that makes you wish it had been the first page of a new report focusing entirely on YLD. The Bank runs the Development Gateway which every month sends out the DG Alerts 'Youth for Development' – 20-30 news flashes on issues relating to youth and development. Since August 2004 I have received 1,457 pieces of information from that source – surely the most comprehensive accumulation of data about youth and development in the world. Here are some examples:

- **Why Pumping Water is Child's Play:** 25 April 2005 (BBC) – A company in South Africa has found a way to harness youthful energy in solving the perennial problem of water supply in rural villages. Playground roundabouts linked to water pumps![2]

- **Seeds of Peace – helping young leaders:** Founded in 1993, Seeds of Peace is dedicated to empowering young leaders from regions of conflict with the leadership skills required to advance reconciliation and coexistence. Read *The Olive Branch*, the magazine of Seeds of Peace, written and edited by youth;[3]

- **Hoops 4 Hope – Youth Development Through Life Skills and Sports:** Hoops 4 Hope is a not-for-profit organization that supports youth development in Zimbabwe and South Africa by working with schools, shelters, and community organizations. Hoops 4 Hope provides the most basic tools that young people need to play team sports.[4]

The World Bank's inspiring leadership in raising the profile of youth in development cannot be overemphasised. Their 2007 World Development Report entitled *Development and the Next Generation* is only the most visible evidence of its support. The former President of the World Bank, James Wolfensohn, was voted a 'Champion of Youth' at the 2005 World Youth Congress in Stirling, Scotland, for speaking out so powerfully in support of youth as an actor in the development process. Not only did he initiate the WDR, he also put considerable effort into setting up the UN Youth Employment Network, the World Bank's Children and Youth Department – and creating policies that require young people to be consulted in every Bank initiative. Though the Bank's execution of the Wolfensohn policies is not all that we – or he – would have hoped, it is an excellent foundation on which to build. Where the Bank leads, other development agencies eventually follow.

International Youth Foundation (IYF)

The biggest grant ever given by the Kellogg Foundation ($65 million) was to Rick Little in 1990 to start the International Youth Foundation. Its founding ethos was to "promote ideas that work". IYF delivers life skills programming to empower young people aged 12-24 to be healthy, productive and engaged citizens. Their programmes currently touch the lives of over 2.2 million young people in 70 countries through a network of visionary partners – corporations, governments, and NGOs. Rick has now moved on to start another organisation. His successor, Bill Reese, has developed within IYF – alongside such excellent programmes as ENTRA 21 (government, civil society and the private sector working to train and place young people in specific jobs needed by employers) – YouthActionNet™, a programme to promote youth-led initiatives. Its stated goal is to "identify and enhance the leadership potential of emerging young leaders". To date, YouthActionNet has trained, mentored and provided grants to more than 100 young social entrepreneurs in 47 countries. The YouthActionNet virtual learning website has attracted more than one million online visitors. After five years of refining the YouthActionNet learning model, IYF is now launching national YouthActionNet Institutes throughout the world to foster a new cadre of engaged young leaders and social entrepreneurs. Each institute will offer young people a 10-12 month fellowship experience, providing small grants, networking opportunities, technical support, and training in advocacy activities from a pro-bono global public relations and media firm.

YouthActionNet piloted its first national institute in Mexico in 2006 with the support of the Sylvan/Laureate Foundation. In 2007, it is expanding to Australia, Haiti, Brazil, and Turkey. In these countries, IYF will create a critical mass of young social entrepreneurs who, individually and collectively, represent a powerful force for good. This global web of leadership learning institutes will raise global awareness about the power and promise of youth-led change.

IYF recently published *Our Time is Now*, a collection of inspirational stories of the achievements of young people in development. Bill Reese writes in his introduction:[6]

"My admiration and sincere thanks go out to all those young people who agreed to share their stories with us and with the world. You humble and inspire us with your passion and your dedication to improving the lives of others."

Archbishop Desmond Tutu continues:

"Youth are uniquely equipped to change the world because they dream. They choose not to accept what is but to imagine what might be. These young visionaries are representatives of thousands of their peers in communities large and small around the globe. So what are the lessons we can learn from them? First – that every individual has the power to make a difference. Second – is to recognise the growing contribution being made by today's youth in making the world a better place. Young people are taking action like never before. This is good news for all of us. And the final, critical lesson is the vital role that each of us can play in supporting youth-led efforts – the non-profit leaders, the business people, the government officials and community members who rallied behind these leaders offering their time, their expertise, their financial support and encouragement. The partnership is all – and today's global challenges have the capacity to bring us closer together than ever before!"[7]

Here are some of the stories:[8]

• **The Meena Clubs** – empowering young women. Jyoti Mohapatra was 19 when she returned to her village and was reminded of the discrimination against women in Indian society. Young women were initially reluctant to come to her meetings – but by the time she left, 60 were attending regularly. The club was named after the character in a UNICEF cartoon, Meena, a young woman who takes on leadership roles. The clubs caught on – and there are now more than 300 across Orissa State. According to state authorities, the clubs 'help to improve the living conditions in their communities in areas such as health, nutrition and education.' Their goal is simply to make women recognise that they are the equal of men – and one of the ways they do this is NOT to have elected leaders in their groups. All members are equal. A unique organisation created out of the unique mind of a unique young person.

• **ATM – Action for Teenage Mothers** In Kenya, more than 1,000 teenage girls become pregnant every day, generally through a lack of sex education. Stella Amojong saw a friend of hers being thrashed and told to shut up by her mother for asking questions about her sexuality. Another friend died after having an illegal abortion – a common occurrence, as 500 of that 1,000 try to get rid of their babies by any means. Stella started by founding 'Girl-Power' – a group dedicated to circulating SRH information amongst its members through plays, seminars, and talks – all given by young people. As her work grew and spread to other slum areas, she developed new projects and got more assistance from IYF and others. Her project 'Compassion' seeks to prevent the spread of HIV-AIDS while supporting those infected with the disease with home help. 'Wind of Hope' provides young mothers with tutoring, career counselling and assistance in getting their secondary school certificates.

• **The Omid Centre, Afghanistan** Sadiqa Basiri was quite lucky to have fled from her homeland to Pakistan at a young age. In Pakistan, she was able to go to school – where in her home village, the Taliban would have prevented her. 'Omid' means hope in Farsi – and that was what Sadiqa brought back to her village when she returned. Now, the Omid centre has 27 teachers and 1,100 female students who had never seen the inside of a classroom. She has been supported to set up three other schools – and dreams of setting up girls' schools across Afghanistan. She is not yet 25!

• **The Oaktree Foundation, Australia** Hugh Evans was voted Young Australian of the Year in 2004 and is the beneficiary of several World Vision grants. Hugh had seen the poverty of his peers in India and South Africa. In his time as a volunteer, he had formed strong friendships – and learned a lot from the young people whom he was supposed to help, but who were, in fact, helping him get his life coordinates right. He started the Oaktree Foundation to ensure that 'fortunate' Australians understand their comparative prosperity – and get involved in the business of making a better world. To date, the Foundation has mobilised more than 3,000 volunteers and supporters, raised $400,000 and established offices in Australia, the USA, UK and South Africa. It supports youth-led poverty eradication projects in more than 20 countries – mostly in the South and West Pacific area. Tim Costello, CEO of World Vision Australia, writes: "Hugh Evans's enthusiasm, passion, dedication and ability to take on any challenge thrown his way epitomises all we could hope for in the youth of our nation." Congratulations to World Vision for finding and nurturing him! Now let's hope that they, and other development agencies, will become true Champions of Youth and invest in the thousands of other Hugh Evans who exist out there, waiting to be supported and nurtured.

• **Intepay, Argentina** Maria D'Ovidio was 22 when she heard Mohammed Yunus speak about creating a 'World without Poverty'. She persuaded her father to send her to Bangladesh to study the practice of the Grameen Bank in helping impoverished women haul themselves out of poverty through micro-credit loans. Returning to Buenos Aires, she set up Intepay ('Sunlight' in the Quechua language). Her programmes have brought work and dignity to 150 workers in projects ranging from candle-making to silk-screening, design and knitting. "I love what I do," says Maria. "The hardest thing is to change the mentality of people who don't trust themselves or others. I have to spend a lot of time to build trust with them – a process of constant construction."

• **Action E-3 on AIDS** The three 'E's John Ckukwudi Bako refers to in the title of his organisation are Education, Enlightenment and Eradication. By official estimates, one in 20 Nigerians is infected with HIV. Some 1.5 million have died of it – and another 1.5 million orphans have been created by it. For John, there is no more urgent issue facing his country. Action E-3 uses a variety of creative means to communicate the key messages about HIV-AIDS – through radio, the internet, football personalities, songs, and dramatic performances of popular folk-tales. HIV-AIDS infection rates are now falling in Nigeria, and the stigma associated with having the disease is reducing. But John is not complacent. He used to dream of being a diplomat and joining a foreign embassy. No more! "All I think of and dream about is how to curb the spread of HIV-AIDS which threatens to tear apart the social fabric of my country."

• **Disabled Children Parents Association (DCPA), Kyrgyzstan** Though founded by her mother, wheelchair-bound Seinep Dyikanbaeva is the voice of DCPA. "Disability is not the obstacle," she says. "The real problem is poor public health services, discrimination, stigmatisation and the absence of resources. I do not see myself as disabled. I see myself as a full member of society." In a three-room office, 20 volunteers work to empower disabled children and their parents to take charge of their lives by offering counselling, therapy, field trips, seminars and holidays. It has done media events, built a rehabilitation centre for 40 youth to give guidance and support for disabled youth and their families. Seinep's goal is "to show the positive side of the lives of the disabled". Still only 20, Seinep takes her leadership role seriously: "I am an example to our young members. I feel responsibility for how I behave and cope with my problems. Every day, I try to be more positive, more responsible, and more trustworthy."

Ashoka Youth Ventures

Currently working in 11 countries, Youth Venture[9] was started by the charismatic Bill Drayton, the former McKinsey consultant who founded Ashoka. Bill has clocked up a good number of success stories, and he believes that young people are to development what women were 30 years ago: invisible – unacknowledged, under-supported and thus contributing a small fraction of what they could contribute. Youth Venture envisions a world where everyone is a change maker – a global culture of young people initiating positive social change. Youth Venture's mission is to build a global movement of young people being powerful now, change makers now – in the present, not just the future. This is the foundation of the 'Everyone a change maker' world – the key factor for success in every society, organisation and person. Bill says:

> "Youth Venture is the civil rights movement for young people. We want every young person to know that if they have an idea and they create a team, we're with them to help them succeed. Any young person who has had that experience knows that they are powerful. They are empowered to go and do anything. They know that they have changed their world – not in a simulation or a game, but the real thing. They have put in place a tutoring system, a dance academy

with peer-counselling, sports that weren't there before, radio programming . . .
it doesn't matter what it is: it's their idea, their team, their impact. They're going
to try it again and again, they're going to get better at it. They're going to get
stronger. What we're building up to is a change in the whole dynamic – the
whole understanding of what the youth years are about. Instead of saying:
'Adults are in charge of everything', we say – you take the initiative! If we can go
from two to three percent of the population becoming natural leaders to 50-60
percent in the next generation, just think what a difference that will make –
both in the lives those young people go on to live – and in the health and creativity of our whole society!" [10]

Youth Venture inspires and invests in young people to launch their own
social ventures and connects them to a powerful network of young change
makers around the world. Youth Venture provides the teams with tools and
resources to help them launch and lead their ventures, seed funding, ongo-
ing coaching and support, adult allies and technical allies who provide
expertise, media, local fellowship events, and participation in a powerful
global fellowship. It currently operates in the US, Mexico, Argentina, Brazil,
India, South Africa, Thailand, France, Germany and Spain but has plans to
expand into several more.

Examples of Youth Ventures include:[11]

• **Team Revolution** is a youth centre that provides recreation and leadership opportunities for teens in Brooklyn. Started by Divine and his team-
mates Deandra, Jamaal and Fernando, Team Revolution has been
recognised as 'redefining volunteerism'. This year they performed in a post-
game Super Bowl concert.

• **Kids Who K.A.R.E. (Kids Autism Research Effort)** was started by
Jessica, Rachel and Ngiste to dispel stereotypes about young people with
autism. They have published a series of illustrated educational children's
books about mental disabilities, which they distribute to local schools and
libraries.

• **Students United for Racial Equity (SURE)**, started by Nina, has created
a syllabus-based 14-session seminar on race issues for high school students, demonstrated first in five California schools as a pilot for national
replication.

- **SIPACSA, Chennai**: Vipin, Nancy, and Alankaar launched SIPACSA (School-based Intervention for Preventing & Addressing Child Sexual Abuse) to address the 'untouchable' issue of child sexual abuse in families in Chennai, India. Their workshops raise awareness, break myths, and above all, tell children that if they have been abused, it's not their fault. They have a waiting list of schools in Chennai wanting their programme.

- **Pukaar**, Mumbai: Sameer and Rajesh, two former street kids, have formed Pukaar to offer food, shelter, rights training, vocational training and health services to young street kids. In the last year, this network has enabled 50 youth to permanently move off the streets.

- **Jivan Dan**, Assam-Nagaland borders: Gerald works to liberate adivasis (indigenous people) from the stranglehold imposed on them by money-lenders to whom they have mortgaged their land. Through training adivasi youth, mentoring young farmers, and working with the adivasi community to address their problems proactively, Gerald is sharing solutions with farmers who currently cannot see beyond their problems.

- **Chamna Thuptep**, Manipur: Chamna Thuptep means 'promises of peace.' Having grown up with conflict, Rebecca Haokip is confident that youth can lead the way to peace. She mobilises youth in villages into 'peace cells' and trains them to organise peace workshops in their communities.

- **Dhritii** was founded by Nidhi Arora, Anirban Gupta, Arindam Dasgupta to inspire, support and spread a culture of entrepreneurship in Indian society through training workshops and individual initiatives at multiple levels.

- **Save Satpuda**, set up by Vishal Bansod and Pratap Thakare, works to conserve the critical wildlife region of Satpuda in Central India. It seeks to conserve the forests while ensuring that the land rights of the tribal people, who depend on the forests for survival, are protected. Save Satpuda works in education, conservation and research.

- **JOMEC (Jóvenes Micro Emprendedores de Cocina)** Started by three young Mexicans to address nutritional deficiencies, JOMEC is a cookery school and catering service for young people and families.

- **RAPEM (Rap Pandillero Estilo Mexicano)** appears to outsiders as a school for rap; inside, it is a safe, non-violent centre to bring together gangs, let them express their concerns and desires, and change society's perception of urban gang youth.

In some ways, the main Ashoka Fellows[12] programme provides an even better model for Youth-led Developers to follow. Bill and his colleagues around the world seek out and celebrate individuals (not just young people) who have blazed a trail with a new idea – a social invention that genuinely creates change in communities and countries. A board reviews each nomination and, if accepted, they are supported with money and trained with entrepreneurial skills by McKinsey and other consultants from the private sector. Bill says: "There is nothing so powerful in the world as a new idea in the hands of an entrepreneur." And the Ashoka Fellows community now has close to 2,000 members. What is clear from meeting them is that they all draw immense inspiration, support, ideas and leverage from their membership of the Ashoka Community. Being able to rub shoulders with celebrity social entrepreneurs like Mohammed Yunus of the Grameen Bank or Ami Dar,[13] the founder of Idealist.com, is incredibly helpful and supportive. The power of networking, of sharing ideas and supporting each other to be ever more creative within this already creative community is a powerful idea. A goal of the Youth-led Development movement is to create an equally strong and mutually supportive network of young development experts – sharing ideas and supporting each other to be successful. Youth Venture is doing just that by connecting young Venturers around the world in a global fellowship of like-minded youth. Through its website (www.genv.net) it has created an online community for young change makers from all over the world to interact with each other, exchange ideas, support each other, and perhaps even collaborate.

Be the Change! – Youth-led Development Programme[14]

My own initiation into the world of Youth-led Development was entirely unlooked for. Peace Child had launched an initiative to draw up young people's priorities for the new millennium at a World Youth Congress to be held on the eve of the millennium in October 1999. Dutifully, the young participants, millions of them around the world, drew up their priorities and surprised us by concluding that education should be the world's top priority going into the new millennium. More important than this was their insistence that they should not just be educated about their planet's descent into misery and environmental death. Rather, they should be trained, equipped and financed to address the problem themselves – to "be the change they want to see in the world", in Gandhi's famous line. In the years since, we have struggled to scrape together enough funding to test the hypothesis that YLD provides the biggest bang for any development buck. In eight years, we have received thousands of proposals and been able to fund about 10 percent of them. Here are some examples:[15]

• **Nairobi, Kenya – Tough Cookie** We funded Florence Wanjuku to set up a bakery school for single mothers in the Kibera slum. Her cookies were delicious – and they are now selling them on street corners across the city, making money for the mothers, and giving them – and their babies – a hopeful future.

• **Harbou, Cambodia – School Fish Pond** Children were dropping out of the school in droves because there was no food for school lunches. So the students decided to create a fish farm. They dug a huge pond and stocked it with local fish. Not only did the students return and eat great fish dinners, they learned a lot about the mechanics and science of fish-farming too!

• **Rukhala, Kenya – Well and Water Pump** In western Kenya, on the shores of Lake Victoria, life is harsh. There are many HIV-AIDS orphans, and victims of malaria: clean water is in short supply, so we funded the village youth association to dig a well and install a pump. The first well they dug struck brackish water. Undeterred, the youth dug a second, then a third where they struck sweet water. They built the surround in concrete, sank the pipe and fixed up the pump. Not only did they make money from villagers only too willing to pay for it, they noticed that the number of patients at the local health clinic dropped by half in the first month following installation. With a second grant, they installed irrigation pipes which started a whole horticultural enterprise that now employs most of them.

• **Paraja Galarza, Corrientes, Argentina – Sanitary/Health Centre** Our grant triggered matching grants worth three times the size of what we gave. This allowed this tiny village to build and equip a health centre in the middle of a rural region with the poorest social indicators in Argentina.

• **Freetown, Sierra Leone – Mandela Toilets** In the Mandela camp for 1,000 internally displaced persons there are only seven toilets: pit latrines of the most squalid variety with the sewage flowing down open gulleys in front of the houses. For years the authorities promised to do something about it, but James Koruma and his friends decided that they would 'be the change' they wanted to see in their community and accepted a grant of $1,000 from us. They bought a pipe, bought the sanitary ware and cement, built new toilets, and ran a pipe down the middle of the street to take the sewage out of the open gulleys and down to the main city sewer. Smell reduced, people happier, youth empowered! (see photograph in centre pages).

Reading through the files of these projects once more for this study, I am reminded of the blurred photographs of the first motorcars, with a man walking in front with a red flag to warn pedestrians! These are the very first, faltering steps in the YLD movement. It is hard to discern from these examples what the Bentley Continental or – more appropriately – the Toyota Prius of YLD efforts might be in future. Because there is no investment, no research, no proper evaluation, training or guidance, it is a miracle that any of these projects get completed at all. With the proper support infrastructures in place, and an education system that rewards concrete project achievement in a similar way to written exams and essays, young people will amaze us with what they can achieve both in the fields of social enterprise as promoted by IYF, Ashoka and BTC, and in the field of youth-led business start-ups championed by the Prince's Trust, YBI and others.

UNIDO[16]

UNIDO Director-General Kandeh Yumkella has given enormous support to the concept of Youth-led Development through job creation, first by organising a ministerial breakfast on the issue during the 2006 ECO-SOC gathering in Geneva, then by hosting an experts' working group meeting on the issue in Vienna, followed by a high-level meeting in Accra, Ghana, in partnership with UNDP, ILO and the African Union. His own personal championship of youth employment is evident from his opening statement:[17]

"I flew 20 hours to be here from Delhi as I believe this issue is important. There is nothing new about Youth Employment in this region – I know this. We have all talked about it too much! For too long, we have disappointed the youth and undervalued their solutions to the problem. In presenting their programme to this august meeting, the youth have said, and I quote:

'We thank the UN for all the reports that have laid out the problems faced by our generation in this region – the high unemployment and illiteracy rates; the poor infrastructure; the mediaeval regulatory environment; the problems of rural youth; the links between youth employment and regional security; the gulf between paper policy intentions and the funds to implement them. We both know these problems, so we do not intend to repeat them... Rather we intend to outline a practical Plan for Actions to solve them.'[18]

He said of the young in West Africa's trouble spots: "Unless we find them real jobs, these kids will head north."

UNIDO has now developed a full, costed Programme of Action 2008–2012 which retains many of the key elements of the MRU-YEF programme devised by youth of the region. Working with the ILO, UNDP and other UN agencies, it is shaping up to become an excellent example of the UN system 'delivering as one'. It has already attracted significant murmurs of interest from major funding agencies.

IADB – A Roof for My Country and other MIF initiatives

The Inter-American Development Bank's Multilateral Investment Fund (MIF)[19] has invested some $300 million dollars in youth-related projects over the past 10 years. One of them is, to my mind, the most impressive Youth-led Development project of all. It even got a well-deserved mention in the World Bank Development report. Called Un Techo para Mi País (A Roof for my Country), it was founded in 1997 by a group of Chilean university students. Their website[20] bristles with the fantastic impatience and idealism of youth engaged on a passionate mission.

"We are a dynamic institution comprised of young people who refuse to ignore the realities in our region: more than 208 million people in Latin America living in extreme poverty – people who have never been given the opportunity or support to build their own paths in life. We hold the conviction that a more fair world is possible and we are willing to do whatever it takes to change the face of Latin America, a continent riddled with inequality. We are young people who are finally taking action throughout Latin America and we will not allow the poor to keep waiting. 'Un Techo Para Mi Pais' works with the poorest families in our respective countries – first to construct emergency houses and then develop integrated programs of social development in areas such as education, micro-credit, job training and community development. We are determined to generate a social conscience in Latin America so that the youth become a part of common fight against corruption, populism, and demagogy. To be able to accomplish our goals we look to incorporate people who believe that poverty is everyone's problem. We look for those who will not allow the poor to keep waiting."

Their methodology consists of selecting target encampments based on the most severe poverty indicators and the urgency of their housing needs. An agreement is reached with families for their participation in the housing construction itself, along with a contribution of 10 percent of the building costs. Community help is also enlisted, and in some cases municipalities cooperate by providing materials and logistical support. In this way, residents, local government and community groups feel ownership of the project.

During construction, the students take care to develop residents' skills and qualifications through on-the-job training in trades such as plumbing, electricity, food services, business administration and access to credit for the promotion of micro-enterprises, mainly in the areas of health, education and legal aid.

Since the beginning, A Roof for My Country has built more than 24,000 basic housing units and recruited more than 18,000 volunteers with the goal of securing minimum living conditions for low-income people to enable them to break out of the cycle of poverty. Today, the project has reached Uruguay, Argentina, Mexico, Peru, El Salvador and Colombia.

AISEC: It's Up to You![21]

What began in 1948 as an organisation to help develop "friendly relations" between member countries, is now is the world's largest student organisation, present in 100 countries. It is also the world's largest youth-led organisation that we have been able to identify, entirely run by students and recent graduates of institutions of higher education. The organisation is headed by a rotating president, elected by the membership. The post is currently held by 24-year-old Gabriela Albescu from Romania.

Today, AISEC takes a pro-active role in developing self-awareness and a personal vision amongst young people, building networks, and developing capacity to drive change.

AISEC values [22] are an excellent articulation of the core values of YLD:

- **Activating Leadership** AISEC staff lead by example and inspire leadership through action and results. We take full responsibility for our role in developing the potential of all people.

- **Demonstrating Integrity** We are consistent and transparent in our decisions and actions. We fulfil our commitments and conduct ourselves in a way that is true to our identity.

- **Living Diversity** We seek to learn from the different ways of life and opinions represented in our multicultural environment. We respect and actively encourage the contribution of every individual.

- **Enjoying Participation** We create a dynamic environment by active and enthusiastic participation of individuals. We enjoy being involved in AIESEC.

- **Striving for Excellence** We aim to deliver the highest quality performance in everything we do. Through creativity and innovation we seek to continuously improve.

- **Acting Sustainably** We act in a way that is sustainable for our organisation and society. Our decisions take into account the needs of future generations.

AISEC is a big international platform, with 22,000 student members where young people discover and develop their potential so as to have a positive impact on society. Its programmes provide more than 5,000 leadership positions to its young members, usually doing internships in large companies. It also delivers more than 350 conferences and runs exchange programmes that enable more than 4,000 students and recent graduates to live and work in another country.

Free the Children (FTC) [23]

Free The Children calls itself "the largest network of children helping children in the world", with more than one million youth involved in 45 countries. It is both funded and driven by children and youth. FTC's mission is to free young people from the idea that they are powerless to bring about positive social change, by encouraging them to act now to improve the lives of young people everywhere. Founded by Craig Kielburger when he was just 12 years old, FTC has an established track record of success, with three nominations for the Nobel Peace Prize and partnerships with the United Nations and Oprah's Angel Network.

"FTC promotes the asset-based community development (ABCD) model which asserts that sustainable development must be community-led. At the heart of the ABCD approach lies the belief that local, indigenous people – their institutions, skills and capabilities – are the most critical resources for sustainable development."

Programmes: To help free children from poverty and exploitation, FTC implements four specific Education for All Children programmes to help children reach their full potential:

1. School building Providing the schools, teachers, and resources disadvantaged children need to get a basic primary education. FTC has built 450 primary schools in 16 developing countries, attended by more than 40,000 children every day. Education is where social and economic development begins – the key to breaking the cycle of poverty and ending the exploitation of children. This is why FTC adds new schools every month. Every school is customized to the area, depending on the size, location and needs of the community. To build, sustain, and monitor the schools, FTC works with reputable local partners and with on-site FTC representatives. Many of the schools are built with the help of volunteers. At least 50 percent of children attending Free The Children schools are girls who would otherwise be working as marginalised child labourers in exploitative conditions.

2. Alternative Income Around the world, many young children cannot go to school because they have to work to help support their families. In areas of low employment, poverty is the normal state of affairs, and parents do not have the skills or the money to provide properly for their children. Children have no choice but to help the family; the alternative is starvation. Recognising that parents want to provide for their children, FTC implements alternative income projects that give those disadvantaged families a sustainable source of income. To date, Free The Children's Alternative Income Campaign has directly benefited more than 22,500 people in Asia, Latin America and Africa. Alternative Income projects include sustainable agricultural initiatives, purchase of animals and machinery for struggling farmers along with support for women's cooperatives.

3. Health Care, Water, and Sanitation This programme puts health kits, clinics, wells, and other critical pieces into place so that children get proper care and maintain their health. Free The Children is committed to helping communities become self-sufficient and meet their basic health care needs. FTC supports a number of health care projects which allow families to lead healthy and productive lives. To date FTC has shipped more than $11 million worth of medical supplies. It has also built health care clinics in Asia, Latin America and Africa, benefiting more than 505,000 people.

4. Peace building Free The Children believes that young people are the key to peace. Thus the organisation has developed a number of activities that promote peace and understanding among young people at the local, national and international level. Working in partnership with the United Nations Special Representatives for Children and Armed Conflict, Free The Children is leading a series of campaigns to raise awareness and help war-affected children, including:

• Schools for Peace

• War is Not A Game

• Peace Ambassadors

• Peace Centers

• Peace Education Tour

Kenya Education Partnerships (KEP)[24]

KEP's aim is to improve secondary school education for young people in south-west Kenya around the town of Kisii. It was started by students at Oxford and Cambridge Universities, and demonstrates the care and thoroughness that young people can bring to development efforts. British students from KEP work in direct partnership with the schools – developing their capacity for self-led growth through equipping them with library books and equipment, for their science laboratories. A small percentage is spent on improving the physical infrastructure of schools where absolutely necessary and on running events such as sports days, health information days and careers events. In 2006, Kenya Education Partnerships directly invested more than £20,000 in 10 rural schools. Every summer, KEP recruits 20 students from British universities and sends them to Kenya to work with the schools to purchase resources, help with school management and implement guidance and counselling for students.

• **The Problems** Students attending rural schools in Kisii have been faced with the challenge of learning and taking exams without any science equipment or books. Generally there is one core text book per subject, used only by the teacher, and by exam time students will probably have only watched one or two science experiments, even though conducting science practicals remains an integral component of the national exams.

• **Unqualified Teachers** Many teachers are unqualified. Often students complete their final school year only to return the next year to teach.

• **Delayed Progression** Because exams happen at harvest time and students are taken out of school to help, some get 'stuck' in a year, perhaps taking eight to 10 years to complete a single year. In some KEP schools, we find students over 25 years old!

• **The Lunch Programme** If a school does not provide lunch, pupils will often not return after going home for lunch.

• **Gender Inequalities** Girls are a minority in many rural schools – through teenage pregnancy and the family preference to educate boys.

KEP's Strategy: KEP works with the most under-resourced secondary schools in the Kisii region. In theory, every secondary school in Kenya should be provided by the government with sufficient qualified teachers and suitable resources. In practice, schools are given very limited resources and are understaffed, and so are forced to source and pay for their own, often unqualified teachers, or to go without resources completely. KEP trains and empowers their selected schools to raise funds through community fund-raising events and book donation days. By careful collection of school fees, KEP aims to lead their schools on to a path of self-led, sustainable improvement. The strategies include:

• **Resource investment** KEP annually recruits and trains a team of 20 students to design and implement resource acquisition programmes to help the schools to achieve a sustainable level of growth, from which they can then manage their own expansion. Only sustainable resources are purchased – such as books, science equipment, furniture and sports equipment. KEP does not provide money for buildings.

• **Active partnership:** Volunteers go out during their summer vacation, working in pairs to invest up to £2,000 in resources over their eight-week stay. This means each school will typically receive between £4,500 and £7,500, and the school's intake of pupils will generally increase from around 100 to 300 students over the three to five year active partnership period. The school also increases its revenue from the increased number of pupils paying fees, and from the money it receives from the government.

• **Post-programme support:** after the period of support, each programme school receives an annual visit from a senior KEP representative to monitor progress on matters of school development. In this way, KEP support and guidance never ends: the school has a friend and mentor for life!

• **Partnering with the right schools:** KEP focuses on schools that have the potential to continue "growing after we have finished investing in them". This means schools with efficient, dynamic management; the strong support of the local community and the potential to increase enrolment.

Conclusion

If you have read this far, I hope that you are now groaning under the weight of evidence of the success and potential of Youth-led Development. I could go on – and probably should, as I haven't mentioned yet the amazing Youth-led project work done by Plan International, Raleigh International, VSO, United Games, EVS, GYAN, Envie d'Agir, GYSD, Zivildienst, the US Peace Corps, Fredskorpset, Canada World Youth, the Commonwealth Youth Programme, the European Commission Youth dept., Norwegian People's Aid, the Nordic Council – not to mention each of the thousands of youth-led business start-ups supported by the Prince's Trust, YBI, Trickle-up and all the other micro-credit initiatives that have supported young people in their first investment ventures. But – enough already! This is not an encyclopaedia! One day, there will be a website that will compare and contrast the experiences of all young people who do YLD projects in all the different areas, so that we can all learn from each other's mistakes and build that Prius model of Youth-led Development.

Before we do that, though, there needs to be some rigorous academic evaluation of what we have all been up to. Most reporting and evaluation of youth-led projects that I have read has been commissioned by the organisations that funded the projects. My own organisation is likewise guilty: we would say that our programmes work, wouldn't we? I have been trying to get the EU and others to sponsor independent research into YLD for years – but no one is, as yet, sufficiently interested. Certainly young people themselves are far more interested in doing the projects than conducting lengthy evaluations of what actually happened. As soon as one project is over, the natural inclination of youth appears to be to move on, as quickly as possible, to the next project.

So – in the Co-management equation – research is the perfect role for the elders: the government ODA agencies, the think tanks, the development professionals who can observe and articulate how YLD practise may be improved. And, much as we may rage against the excesses of the corpulent, elder-led development sector, YLD very much needs their partnership and support. For if we are serious about getting that 0.7 percent of ODA – that $500-$750 million into the YLD sector by 2010, there is a serious problem of absorptive capacity. Channels do not exist in the YLD field to cope with that kind of funding. We shall have to work through the infrastructure of the big agencies to support and manage the money for the young people of the networks we will set up.

The partnership is all! Young people are currently outside the professional development loop, banging on the doors, begging to know: 'How can we help?' For years, the professional development agencies have slammed the door in their faces, saying in so many words: 'You can't!' That, at least, is young people's perception of their response. The evidence provided here should at least be sufficient to prove that this is not an appropriate answer. As more and more students in Europe and North America line up to do gap year voluntary service in developing countries, and more and more unemployed graduates of developing world universities cast around for support to start their own businesses or social infrastructure projects, the elders of the development industry must open that door a snitch and welcome in the leaders of the YLD community for a constructive dialogue on the question: how can we tap into the talent, energy and hope of the world's three billion young people to Make Poverty History and achieve the Millennium Development Goals?

The form that this research takes is critical. In the final chapter, I shall outline the policy frameworks I have developed over a number of years in partnership with a network of West African youth NGOs which, I believe, articulate an infrastructural approach which will enable a nationwide YLD programme to impact every single young person in a small country like, say, Sierra Leone, Guinea or Liberia. The impact of such a programme should be discernable after a year – but the real proof of its effectiveness would be five to 10 years into the programme. Longditudinal research programmes need to be set up in parallel on the Action Research model. But other programmes should not wait: we can start effective programmes in all 50 LDCs by 2010. Young people in all these countries should be engaged as soon as possible. They should be trained and supported on the basis of the analysis of the first one or two years' work in the pilot countries. And each of them should be subject to the same, rigorous Action Research evaluations of the pilot countries.

By 2010, all ODA agencies should be persuaded that YLD makes sense and want to join us in making it a top priority for ODA investments up to 2015. Only in that way will we get close to achieving the Millennium Development Goals in these countries – and, more important, lay the foundations for a successor campaign to eradicate poverty by 2030.

Control Group Research

The evidence of success described in this chapter must suggest that a wider programme of research into YLD is essential. We request that it be Action Research [25] – research done on the job. Do not make the young people wait any longer: give them a chance to prove that they can make poverty history.

However, development economists argue that genuinely compelling research requires control groups: you find a village and embed a YLD programme in it. The local/international volunteer mentors will be in place, business incubators, support networks etc. Also, there should be a sizeable project fund to spend on Social Enterprises, Youth-led Public Works, Youth-led Business Start-ups etc. A second village is then chosen as the control group. Here no similar investments are made. Life continues as normal and direct comparisons between the two after one, two and five years will demonstrate the efficacy, or not, of the YLD investments.

Many youth find it distasteful to condemn a control group community to five years of abject poverty just so that some bean-counting economist can prove that YLD is effective. On balance, though, it is a small price to pay to get the development community's billions flowing into YLD.

Chapter Four

The Imperative of Service

"Service is the rent you pay for room upon this earth!" – **Shirley Chisholm, US Congress**[1]

Youth-led Development is rooted in the idea of service – youth serving society for community benefit rather than their own personal benefit. The imperative of service has been placed on the shoulders of young people since the dawn of civilisation: young people were expected to tend the flocks, milk the cows, gather the harvests. For most children, the experience of childhood was the experience of service. And, of course, the pinnacle of service was the understanding that your king, mogul, chief or emperor could call on you to fight and die for whatever he in his wisdom decided was in the national interest. Few, if any, young people had any choice in the matter: *dulce et decorum est pro patria mori* they were told, and off they went, often to die in their millions.

It was, perhaps, the image of wave after wave of young men being mown down as they stepped over the top of First World War trenches that forced people to think of alternative forms of service to the military. Alternative forms had always been around. In their excellent study of *Service Without Guns*,[2] Don Eberly and Reuven Gal draw attention to the fact that the armies of old Egypt built monuments to their leaders that still stand. Ancient Inca armies built roads and irrigation systems, as did the armies of Rome. Lord Baden Powell saw service to nature, to society, to others, as the foundation of the Scout Movement he founded 100 years ago this year. His Scouts, like many service schemes, drew on the traditions of military organisation. Teams, called variously troops, squads or brigades, emphasised the essential need in any service operation to work as a team. Cooperation, teamwork, working collaboratively, has always been a central component of service, both civilian and military. There is a widespread recognition that either or both forms of service are 'good' for young people. YLD also depends for its success on learning these forms of cooperation and teamwork.

In the UK, the concept of voluntary service is indelibly identified with the great Alec Dickson – founder of Voluntary Service Overseas(VSO) and Community Service Volunteers (CSV). These two organisations remain the backbone of voluntary service in the UK. But though Dickson worked with Sargent Shriver and John F. Kennedy to set up what remains the world's largest and probably most successful international service organisation, the US Peace Corps, the concept of civilian service started in the USA many years before Dickson. John Dewey is credited with coining the phrase 'experiential learning' in his 1938 essay 'Experience and Education'. But it was a Harvard professor, William James, who in 1906 articulated the foundation of current conceptual thinking about civilian service in a lecture entitled 'The Moral Equivalent of War'. In words that recall the 1967 speech of Harold Wilson where he called the War on Want "the only war worth fighting",[3] James called for the "conscription of the whole youthful population to work on the toughest jobs". He argued that those who served would "tread the earth more proudly, be better fathers and teachers of the next generation".[4] Franklin D. Roosevelt was at Harvard at that time and, probably coincidentally, it was he who in 1933 started what still stands in most scholars' minds as the single most successful youth service operation: the Civilian Conservation Corps. It was one of the main initiatives that kick-started the US economy and propelled it out of the Great Depression. It paid young people minimal stipends to plant trees, build nature trails in wilderness areas – and lift them out of the misery of 'nothing-to-do' unemployment. It engaged about 300,000 young people at any one time, and because many of the stipends were sent directly to the volunteers' families, benefited many more depression-hit Americans. It only ended when, with Pearl Harbour, Americans were drawn back into the military.

Since the end of that war, the concept of service has increased and grown across the USA. Kennedy's great contribution was not only the Peace Corps but also VISTA – Volunteers In Service to the Americas. Lyndon Johnson's Great Society initially included the idea of service, until the imposition of the draft for the Vietnam war made the whole idea of service so unpopular that it dropped out of the political vocabulary for a couple of decades. Clinton revived it with his Americorps initiative, which extended the idea of Service Learning. Meanwhile, organisations like Youth Service America and the National Service Learning Conference were promoting the value of service across the USA, setting up service-learning coordinators in many states and education authorities.

At the same time, organisations like the International Baccalaureate[5] were introducing the requirement of Service – CAS (Creativity Activity and Service) – to their examination programme. Each IB student is required to do 200 CAS hours in order to graduate. The University of Costa Rica likewise requires all its students to do community service as a graduation requirement. Medical students in Mexico are required to spend a year bringing basic medical services to remote rural and urban areas before they can apply for salaried jobs in the profession. Nigeria established a National Youth Service Corps (NYSC)[6] after the Biafran Civil War in the 1960s. Administered by the military, it enrols 130,000 university graduates to practise their professions in remote rural areas in return for bed and board. After their year of service, graduates are brought together to reflect on their experiences and discuss how it might be done better.

The reason for the Nigerian initiative was nation-building, healing the rifts amongst the different ethnic groups of that vast country. This goal is common to many service projects and supports the security benefit which I argue is a major reason to invest in YLD. Service activities in Nigeria brought the nation together in a way that no other initiative could do. "I went in to the NYSC as a man from the North, and I came out a Nigerian" said one returning volunteer,[7] achieving exactly the result his government hoped he would achieve. The same ethic informs the EVS initiative of the European Union and the Katimavik initiative in Canada. Katamavik is an Inuit word meaning 'Meeting Place'. The government of Pierre Trudeau started the initiative in 1977 as a response to the Quebecois separatist movement. It brings together teams of 12 young Canadians – four French-speaking, eight English-speaking; six male, six female. Each service team does a series of three-month service projects, living together in Katamavik houses, cooking and cleaning together and going out to work together every day. The programme has ebbed and flowed with the changes in the Canadian government, and has never grown very big. But Quebec has not separated, so perhaps it made a contribution.

Where service programmes overlap completely with YLD programmes is in initiatives like the Literacy Brigades of Cuba and Nicaragua after their respective revolutions. After his 1959 revolution, Castro sent out 100,000 volunteers all over Cuba to teach rural campesinos how to read and write. In spite of a vicious disinformation campaign by the CIA to persuade the campesinos that the teachers were actually foreign agents sent to destroy them (which resulted in several hundred of the Literacy Volunteers being murdered),[8] Castro's initiative reduced the illiteracy rate from close to 30 percent to under five percent in less than a year. A similar effort by the Sandinista government of Nicaragua 20 years later succeeded in halving that country's illiteracy rate from 73 to 37 percent in two years, before the US-led Contra war forced the cancellation of the programme.[9]

It is perhaps a testament to the value and importance of YLD that both centrally planned economies and the world's biggest market economy, the USA, have the world's largest youth service programmes. It is one area where political ideologies evaporate before the overwhelming evidence of the efficacy and value of the programmes. In China, Mao Zedong instilled the idea of service ruthlessly in every sector of society, saying "there is no profound difference between the farmer and the soldier . . ."[10] Indeed, Mao, like Hitler before him, used his armies to build railways and roads, plant trees and clear ground for farming. Now, as the Chinese economy grows apace, volunteerism is still encouraged through schemes like the Chinese Young Volunteers Association, which recruits hundreds of thousands of young people across the country to do service. The All China Youth Federation also organises hundreds of different volunteer initiatives – and a budding environmental movement now boasts more than 2,000 officially registered NGOs, as well as several thousand non-registered groups and environmental businesses. The movement has learned skilfully to navigate the political landscape: 10 years ago, environmental groups tended to focus on the politically neutral issues of environmental education and species protection. They have since grown increasingly bold, influencing government policy and organising protests. Particularly notable was a recent successful campaign by voluntary groups and individuals against dams on the Nu River in Yunnan province.[11]

In the former Soviet Union, volunteerism was encouraged through the youth wings of the Communist party – the young Pioneers and the Komsomol. From the relatively benign 'Subotnik' days – Saturday community clean-ups – to the super-human service of Russian youth to the war effort against the Axis powers, service was engrained in the Soviet mindset. Because it was imposed with such compulsion, young people were only intermittently excited by it. The result was that, when the USSR collapsed, the ideas of volunteerism and service were tossed out along with the Pioneers and the Komsomol in many of the former republics. Throughout the former Soviet bloc, there is a palpable resistance and contempt for any idea of service that smacks of the old Soviet concepts. Shame! It will change but only when the international service opportunities – which form the bedrock of our concept of Global YLD – are sufficiently well established to attract the interest of young Poles, Hungarians, Russians etc.[12]

Finally we come to Europe, where it was the youth service exchanges between Germany and France after the Second World War that laid the social foundations of lasting peace between those two old enemies. It also forged what became the European Union, and inspired our confidence that our Peace Child youth exchanges between the USA and USSR could help bring about the end to the Cold War.

In the years following the Treaty of Rome in 1957, European countries slowly began to discontinue their compulsory military service programmes. Britain was the first to abandon it completely in favour of a professional army. No compulsory service opportunity replaced it. In Germany there is still compulsory service, but increasingly, from the 1960s on, it was the civilian Zivildienst[13] that became the backbone of Germany's service regime, focusing particularly on areas like the care for the elderly.

In Europe today, only four countries – Greece, Turkey, Finland and Switzerland – still demand compulsory military service from their young people. The European Union has picked up the slack by creating the excellent EVS programme that propels young volunteers from every EU member state across the Union in a variety of youth service roles. EVS has just celebrated its 10th anniversary, and extended its service opportunities beyond Europe's borders to other countries of the world. In EVS we get the first constructive experiment in a multinational Peace Corps which lies at the foundation of the Youth-led Development concept proposed in this paper. However, sadly, the department in the European Commission responsible for youth and the one responsible for development have little connection with each other. So the potential for linking the expanded EVS programme and DG Development's programmes has not yet been exploited. (We are working on it!)

As we have seen, concepts of duty and service lie at the heart of YLD. Both have long, rich histories of constructive, concrete and measurable benefit to societies down the centuries. Linking these concepts of service to the wider challenges articulated in the UN's Millennium Development Goals and the realities of fast-depleting natural resources, climate change etc. is what YLD is all about.

Defending the Service-Learning Ethic

With the rise of civil libertarianism later in the 20th century, the idea of even civilian service was challenged through the courts. When the US State of Maryland, along with several US cities, made a period of community service a graduation requirement, civil liberties groups took the State to court on the grounds that such service violated the young people's constitutional rights. The appeal went right up to the Supreme Court where it was, eventually, rejected on the grounds that community service is as much a part of the educational experience as the study of history or mathematics.[14]

A good decision! It gives legal support to the contention I make that YLD is chiefly just another form of education – an essential supplement to class-based teaching. For the international and the local volunteer, YLD is a rounding off of education – an essential way of easing the transition into the world of work. But there is a difference between YLD and normal charitable volunteering: in YLD, there is a strong element of self-interest. The best YLD programmes include either an effective training component that deliver marketable skills, and improve the employability of the young person. Or, in the case of YLBS-Us, they result in income-generating, salary-paying work which delivers concrete financial benefit to the young person who starts them. However, YLD suffers if it is not driven by youthful idealism and a caring altruism for society as well as self. That is why the element of service – volunteerism – is essential to our concept of YLD.

On billboards in Africa, governments call on their citizens to assist in 'nation-building', a call to service that is frequently as incoherent as it is unproductive. Instead, YLD makes a direct call on young people to advance themselves, to improve their skills, support their communities and therefore improve their prospects in life. And it accompanies that call with money, an investment fund, plus a cadre of international volunteers and professional experts who will support them to be successful in achieving their goals.

They have to be motivated to pursue that goal of self-improvement because they want to, not because a government is telling or paying them to. That is the essential foundation of successful YLD – young people getting involved because they want to, because they are motivated for idealistic and other reasons. It is the component that can make the difference between success and failure. And remember, we define success in Nationwide YLD programmes in LDCs as ones that cause the LDC to leap several tens of places up the Human Development Index in a few short years. Failure is defined as policy that produces a generation of disillusioned, feckless, unskilled young people, happy to pick up any gun that any potential revolutionary chooses to offer him or her, or meekly accept the environmental holocaust which nature, in the grip of global warming, may choose to wreak upon them.

"The whole experience was bigger, better, more moving and more perspective-changing than I'd ever expected. I know the individual who benefited most was me, but I think I made a positive impact on the community where I worked. Speaking to my Eritrean teaching colleagues, they'd tell me about VSO volunteers who had taught them years before. They remembered their name, their techniques and character, and always spoke warmly of them. The particular skills I brought home with me were confidence, resilience, patience and a cast iron stomach." – **Sandy Biggar, VSO Volunteer Teacher, Eritrea** [15]

"The generation now being educated will have to do what our generation has been unable or unwilling to do: stabilize a world population which is growing at the rate of quarter of a million each day; stabilize and then reduce the emission of greenhouse gases which threaten to change the climate; protect biological diversity, now declining at an estimated rate of 100-200 species per day; reverse the destruction of rainforests now being lost at the rate of 116 square miles each day; and conserve soils now being eroded at the rate of 65,000,000 tons per day.

Future generations must also learn to use energy and materials with greater efficiency. They must learn to utilize solar energy in all its forms. They must rebuild the economy in order to eliminate waste and pollution. They must learn how to manage renewable resources for the long term. They must begin the great work of repairing the damage done to the Earth in the past 200 years of industrialisation. And they must do all of this while addressing worsening social and racial inequities. No generation has faced a more daunting agenda." – **Professor David Orr, Oberlin College, USA**

Chapter Five

Co-management:
Sharing Responsibility

"Responsibility is the only socially maturing factor." – **Richard Hauser**[1]

"If you give a child responsibility, generally they will behave responsibly: if you deny them responsibility, you cannot then complain if they behave irresponsibly." – **J. S. Mill**[2]

Since International Youth Year[3] in 1985, 'youth participation' has been spoken about, and often included, in official government policies. Youth participation units and officers have sprung up at all levels of government: there are more than 150 Ministries of Youth around the world. Agenda 21 devoted a whole chapter to youth and children, asserting "the right for all young people to be involved in decision-making that affects their future". The UN has a World Programme of Action for Youth[4] which has a section on participation. Even the World Bank has set up a Children and Youth Department – and the Bank's offices are now required to "listen to the voice of youth" before making any investment that affects this sector of the population.

I doubt that many do, and even if they do, few act upon what they hear. For adults instinctively feel they know what's best for young people. They have the experience – the money, the letters after their names, the houses, the mortgages, often the experience of parenting or teaching: it is almost impossible to re-arrange the furniture in older minds to take on the idea that young people should actually be teaching them, giving them instruction, sharing decision-making power with them. Such ideas never occur to the majority of elders. The whole machinery of schooling, compulsorily institutionalising youth for 12 or more years, is only the most obvious indication that adults and governments think they know what's best for young people. And though most schools these days have student councils, their authority rarely strays beyond the canteen menus and leisure events. The idea that young people might actually co-manage what they learn, and con-duct regular assessments on the staff who teach them, as the staff who teach conduct regular assessments of them, is anathema to teachers and their unions.

And, let's be honest, older people are generally a bit jealous of young people. For a start, they are young: they seem to have more fun than we do! They are more attractive than we are, prettier, sexier. They dress better, are more cool – stay up late, sleep in, beat us at sports, go on great holidays, make a lot of noise, have wild parties and, often, they are doing all this with our money! Worst of all, they will still be doing this long after we are dead and in our graves! Why should we defer to them!? You've got to be kidding!

A British youth-worker recently argued that boredom is a new and sub-tle instrument of oppression elders use against youth:

> "Not very long ago, teenagers had no time to be bored. Youth was spent up chimneys, down mines, behind lathes. They may have been exploited in adult business, but at least they were a part of it. They had a purpose. They mattered. Kids today see themselves as under foot, in the way, of no value or interest."[5] A genuine youth participation matters. It creates confident and effective young people.

Real Youth Participation

It doesn't take a cynic to recognise that the great declarations of the last 10 years on 'youth participation' have achieved very little. A seat at the table perhaps; a few words listened to, noted and then forgotten. Youth-led Development requires a much more muscular form of participation. As its name implies, we are talking youth leadership here. Youth-designed, youth-managed, youth-evaluated. But, in developing YLD, it is vital not to allow young people to get carried away with the idea that youth are alone in the world. Of course, they are not – and some of the biggest challenges in real-ising YLD's potential lie in fitting YLD into current political arrangements.

Already there are many remarkable success stories: the Commonwealth Youth Programme has championed youth participation in that organisa-tion loudly and noisily for many years.[6] Its goal has long been "youth main-streaming", which it defines as:

> "... ensuring that young people are a full part of all organisations and all social institutions that make up our societies. Like gender mainstreaming, youth main-streaming seeks to ensure the full citizenship of young people, enabling an

excluded sector of society to become integral into shaping the nature of society through its different social interventions, organisations and institutions. Young people stop being just a target group or beneficiaries, they become integral to the process of finding solutions and implementing those solutions. Youth engagement ceases to be about recruiting young people as volunteers, interns and junior staff members. It is about a deeper transformation that makes them central in the work of the organisation."

However, it has to be agreed that success in most institutions of achieving such high ideals in their political arrangements for young people is patchy. The Commonwealth Secretariat would be the first to agree that their institution has a long way to go. The Council of Europe set up the European Youth Centre and the European Youth Foundation,[7] which organise youth encounters and seminars across the continent. With slightly more verve and a lot more money, the Youth Department of the European Union sets up youth exchanges, voluntary service, and joint trainings of youth workers. Its EVS programme, its Erasmus University exchanges, and its endless research and reflection on youth work and programmes means that it is ahead of the curve in terms of setting up programmes for youth.[8] But though both the European Commission and the Council of Europe promote the concept of youth participation, you will look in vain for young people working in their departments. The Board of the European Youth Centre has representatives of youth bodies in the member states sitting alongside the minister's adult representatives. But inside the secretariat, the staff are all professional elders. In neither organisation have they taken the obvious first step, which would be to allow young people to review and, at the very least, advise on the decisions about which youth projects to fund and which not.

All of which is very strange to an organisation like Peace Child International, which has worked successfully in an equal partnership with young people for close on 25 years. How 'equal' that partnership is questionable: adults own the house in which Peace Child operates and take responsibility for most of the fund-raising, accounts, proposals and report-writing. Only rarely do we find young people who want to work in this area – and, because it takes time to train them in these skills, often they are not around long enough to become very good at it. Yet, as youth make up 12 of the 14 staff – in democratic staff meetings, the youth majority have more than equal say in what projects are pursued and how. So to that extent, we believe our organisation is youth-led.

The 'Ladder of Participation' developed by Dr Roger Hart is a useful shorthand way of defining the different levels of participation. In Peace Child, we have always aspired to the highest level of youth-adult participation and on Hart's graphic, we re-define this as 'co-management', youth and elders becoming equal partners. Other ways may be effective, but for Youth-led Development, a co-management approach is, we feel, the best.

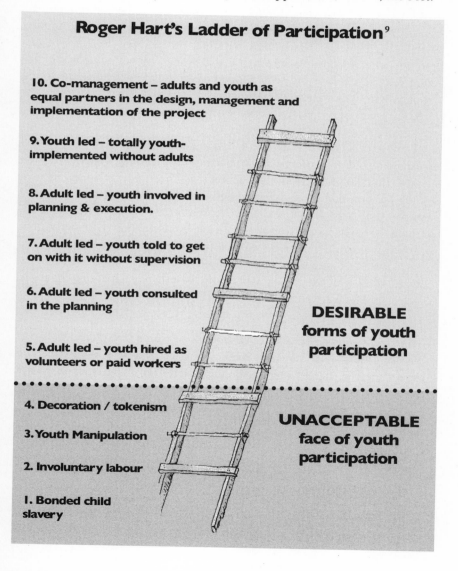

Roger Hart's Ladder of Participation[9]

10. Co-management – adults and youth as equal partners in the design, management and implementation of the project

9. Youth led – totally youth-implemented without adults

8. Adult led – youth involved in planning & execution.

7. Adult led – youth told to get on with it without supervision

6. Adult led – youth consulted in the planning

5. Adult led – youth hired as volunteers or paid workers

DESIRABLE forms of youth participation

4. Decoration / tokenism

3. Youth Manipulation

2. Involuntary labour

1. Bonded child slavery

UNACCEPTABLE face of youth participation

The Peace Child Co-Management Solution

The technology of youth/adult participation and management has always fascinated me. I wrote my Masters' Degree thesis on it at Durham University in 1997.[10] Having practised the technologies for 25 years, I realise how much I have to learn. Most organisations have not reached the first base of understanding that there is in fact a technology to be studied at all. So I knew that I had something to contribute to the field, and when the opportunity of participating in a European Commission project entitled 'Seeking Excellence in Youth Participation at a local level' came up, I gathered five other European Youth NGOs that work with young people in different ways to explore and reflect together on how best adults and young people might work together constructively.

After a year of projects, observations, reports, meetings and reflection, we agreed that 'co-management' is the most effective technology for achieving excellence in youth participation.[11] Co-management may be best explained as old and young people sharing responsibility equally for their successes and failures – working together in a thoroughly business like way, signing Memoranda of Understanding with each other and not requiring each position to be 'shadowed' by a representative of the other side. For example, if a young person is a good webmaster, the co-management approach requires that s/he be allowed to get on with it on his/her own – not shadowed or supervised by an adult – or elder as our vocabulary required us to call the other half of our 'youth participation' equation. (Youth aged 18-25 are adults!)

The hypothesis we sought to test in this project was the following:

> "The way to measure excellence in youth participation with older people is to measure the extent to which the young people feel ownership of the project on which they are engaged and, equally, the extent to which the older people feel satisfied by the contribution being made by the young people."

In every project that we examined in the course of the two years we conducted this research, our hypothesis held true. In Slovenia, the Young Voices group felt complete ownership of the project(s) that the local council funded for them and the political administration felt, on the whole, extremely satisfied with the way that the young people were managing them. When, in local elections, the administration that had set up the participatory processes was defeated and thrown out of office, the new council had considerably less enthusiasm for the projects – demonstrating to the young people the political reality of seeking favour with all political parties not just the one currently in power. In Scotland, where Peace Child organised the 3rd World Youth Congress with the Scottish Executive, our deal was done with the Executive. At our insistence, and with the best of intentions, we engaged the Scottish Youth Parliament (SYP) to set up a Youth Advisory Body to the event. But the SYP felt no ownership of the event – it wasn't their idea. The lavish meetings of the Youth Advisory Board in big hotel rooms felt like efforts to placate the Scottish Youth – rather than to include them. The result was that Scottish Youth felt zero ownership of the progress – and very few Young Scots signed up to come to the Congress. We learned a lot from that: it was the wrong way to go about co-management.

At about the same time, we did a small project to create an info-mercial about sustainable lifestyles with a local school. The young students developed the idea, story-boarded it, acted, filmed, recorded and edited the film – and the adult leadership of Peace Child were extremely pleased with the result. It was excellent proof of our hypothesis.[12]

Our partners in Austria, France, Ireland and Hungary all achieved similar success with their projects, demonstrating to us all that co-management is an excellent way forward in the effort to achieve successful youth participation in decision-making. We say this in all modesty, recognising that some organisations, like AISEC and the European Youth Foundation – and probably others – have achieved significant changes and advances in situations where young people work entirely on their own. But they are the exception that proves the rule, and they confirm the importance of ownership to success.

The business of 'ownership' is vital to YLD: young people are so used to being shaped, manipulated, patted on the head, ordered about, and 'taught' by parents, teachers and others in position of authority that the concept of 'ownership' is very precious to them. Just as successive governments have found, when people own their houses they tend to take better care of them. In the same way, if young people feel ownership of a project or organisation they are working on, they far more likely to give it their best effort than something that they are told to do for a test or some exam qualification.

In the co-management booklet we produced, we explored the possibilities of co-management in many different arenas: in the family, the school, the police and health authorities, in local, national and international government. In each, we suggest that there is a 10-step process that needs to be undertaken to ensure successful partnership between the young people and the elders. One early decision that needs to be taken is where each individual stands on the flexibility chart:

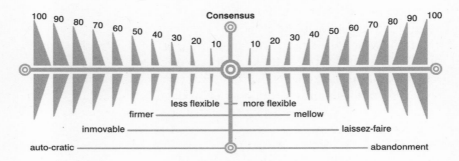

Every person, young and old, has their comfort zone in terms of the authority they like to wield: we have found it helpful to gauge what an individual's comfort zone is like. Likewise, getting adults and youth to open up to each other about their feelings about youth, and vice versa, is immensely helpful. Do adults feel threatened by youth? What do elders do that really irritates youth? Is there a generation gap? What defines it? These, and many other questions, need to be answered to ensure a constructive, harmonious partnership between youth and their elders in each Youth-led Development project. Getting that relationship right, especially between youth and mentors, and between youth and the community they hope to benefit, is essential to success.

"The Millennium Development Goals can be reached but only if we allocate more money to self-help. Every year, $110 billion dollars is given in world aid but only $2 billion goes towards self-help. In south-east Asia, one billion people made it out of poverty, but they didn't do it with aid. We have to replace the giving with lending to business start-ups." – **Percy Barnevik, Business Executive, Adviser to Hand in Hand, India**

Chapter Six

A Policy Framework for a Nationwide YLD Programme

"Confidence between youth and government is currently lacking, making partnership impossible. There has to be engagement of youth in decision-making at the highest level and in civil society, in media, politics, even religion. For our fragmented continent, collaboration with youth organisations will allow the emergence of a new generation of Africans fully conscious of their African heritage and willing to be identified as part of that one, strong nation which is Africa." — **Alpha Bacar Barry, Guinea**

If, 25 years ago, you had asked me which of the world's governments and major international institutions would be the greatest champions of youth, probably the very last one I would have thought of would have been the World Bank! Yet so it has turned out to be. James Wolfensohn, the former World Bank President, devoted about a quarter of his September 23rd 2003 speech to the Bank's Board of Governors to discussing the role of youth in the Bank's affairs. He also joined the Bank to Kofi Annan and the ILO to set up and manage the Youth Employment Network. When setting up the Bank's Children and Youth Department, he ensured that there was an equal focus on children and youth. Crucially, he organised for the 2007 edition of the Bank's World Development Report to focus on the issue of "development for, and by, the next generation."[1]

The Bank's report is a benchmark document for all of us working in this field. Focussed on the economics of the youth sector, and written for economists, it makes the case that "young people today present the world with an unprecedented opportunity to accelerate growth and reduce poverty." In its methodology it surveyed young people, it reviewed all the existing data and, most importantly, its authors took the time and trouble to listen to young people. The thoughts and comments of young people are spattered across every page of the report.

The authors chose to review the data through three 'youth lenses'. First: opportunities for youth. Second: the capabilities of youth. Third: second chances for youth.

Their focus on second chances was very welcome, and economically wise as the cost of remediation is higher for adults than it is for youth. Improving life chances by creating the safety nets for youth who fall foul of the law or drug/alcohol abuse or teenage pregnancy is a very low price to pay for increasing the number of productive adults in society. The authors also raise key dilemmas for policy makers: "When primary school enrolment has gone up so dramatically, why is illiteracy so persistent? Why do large numbers of university graduates go jobless for months, even years, when businesses complain of a lack of skilled workers?" Exactly my point! Without involving youth, investments in youth are not working. Even DfID admits that, in Ghana, where there is now 100 percent enrolment in primary schools, on graduation 43 percent cannot read a line and less than half know how to use a condom. Youth-led peer-to-peer teaching does much better.

I have been trying to get the major ODA ministries and Development NGOs of Europe and the EU's DG Development to develop comprehensive development policies in relation to young people since our first World Youth Congress on this subject in 1999. DfID is something of a bellwether in the European Development Community. If I could get DfID to take the concept of Youth-led Development seriously, I thought there was a good chance that the rest of Europe – and DG Dev. would follow the DfID lead. Now, with the World Development Report, I had the perfect weapon to get the word 'youth' on DfiD's radar!

So it was that I stalked Secretary of State Hilary Benn through several public meetings in the autumn of 2006. Finally, the poor man relented and agreed to discuss the report with his conservative opposite number, Andrew Mitchell, at an All-Party Group meeting on development at the House of Commons, generously co-hosted by ODI, in December 2006. Sadly, his address revealed very little knowledge of the report and even less about the needs of youth: instead, he told anecdotes about his meetings with various inspiring young people in his travels in developing countries. The audience were not impressed. They roasted him, and for the first time, perhaps, he realised that there was a serious institutional vacuum in DfID in relation to the youth sector. The word 'youth' did not appear in the DfID phone book: there was no office in the Palace Street Headquarters with the word 'Youth' on the door! He detailed his staff to look into it.

The Equity and Rights division agreed to plan a networking meeting between DfID and leading NGOs working with youth to explore, initially, a focus on youth employment issues and youth and sexual and reproductive health. The months went by, but finally we were all invited to Palace Street for a meeting of the 'Children and Youth Round Table'.

My heart sank. Once again, officialdom had muddled the children and youth agendas. For all of us who work in the youth field, this has long been a problem: surely it is self-evident that the policy needs of 0-10 year olds are very, very different from the policy needs of 15-24 year olds? Children need protection, special health care, head start and primary school programmes, unconditional love, parenting etc. Youth need employment opportunities, special skills training, participation in decision-making, and support in making the transition from parental dependency to autonomy.

What is particularly galling is that those organisations, like Save the Children, Plan and UNICEF, which look after both children and youth, in fact spend 80-90 percent of their time and resources on the children's issues, leaving the youth issues very much marginalised. The same is true when it comes to government ODA ministries developing policies for children and youth. DfID is in good company when it muddles children and youth: Danida (Denmark),[2] Norway[3] and GTZ (Germany)[4] have, like the World Bank,[5] developed Children and Youth policy statements. Check out the number of times each mentions children (C), youth (Y) and young people (YP):

Name of Organisation & Policy Statement	C	Y	Y P
DANIDA Children & Young People in Danish Development Cooperation	409	62	101
Three Billion Reasons - Norway's Development Strategy for Children and young people in the South	929	26	19
GTZ(Germany) - Children & Youth in Development Cooperation	9	4	12
World Bank - Children & Youth Framework for Action	236	235	34
World Bank - World Development Report 2007	342	1740	839

In the children and youth departments, children always end up getting most of the attention. So you will understand why I was depressed by the DfID approach. However, to its great credit, DfID listened to the wishes of the NGOs and split the group into children and youth pillars, one focused on children, convened by Save the Children, the other focused on youth – convened by Peace Child. It is early days, but all the signs are extremely promising. A secondee has been hired, and a mapping exercise is under way to find out what, if anything, DfID is doing for and with youth. DfID may be behind the Danes, the Norwegians and the Germans, but their commitment to partnership with youth themselves and youth NGOs promises to generate a more ambitious, more youth-friendly youth development policy when it does finally emerge. Thank you, DfID!

In the meantime, it is to the Bank's magisterial World Development Report[6] that we turn for authoritative statements on National Youth Policy. The Report devotes its ninth chapter to the topic. In their analysis, policies directed at youth fail for three main reasons:

- First: Few countries take a coherent approach to establish clear lines of accountability for youth outcomes. Many countries have a vision for young people, typically articulated in a National Youth Policy that fails to set priorities or coordinate action. Even when a policy is well articulated, it may stand alone. Greater capacity is needed, for analysis, for integration with national policy planning and budgeting, for coordinated implementation, monitoring and evaluation.

- Second: Young people often lack voice in the design and implementation of policies that affect them.

- Third: There are too few success stories – few policies and programmes that have proven effective. More needs to be done to find out which policies and programmes improve youth outcomes and why. Knowing what works and what does not and in what circumstances would be of tremendous value in improving youth policy for all countries.

A Comprehensive YLD Policy Framework

It is against this background that I have been involved in development a Nationwide Policy for Youth-led Development[7] for the three countries of the Mano River Union – Sierra Leone, Guinea and Liberia plus Cote D'Ivoire. The framework addresses the three causes of failure identified by the authors of the World Development Report:

1. It seeks a 'coherent approach' by giving ownership to all key stakeholders at government level and including the private sector, civil society, the donor community and the UN agencies ('delivering as one').

2. Young people created the policy: it is their policy created in partnership with experienced development professionals. It is their idea to invite the partnership of all the other stakeholders mentioned above.

3. It seeks to build on the proven success of Youth-led Development. By incorporating serious action research/monitoring/evaluation into each of the programmes, it will build up more evidence of what works and what does not work in the youth/development field to help us win the intellectual argument for YLD.

The framework was developed in partnership with a coalition of some 50 Youth NGOs from the region which suffers from massive youth unemployment (88 percent in Liberia) and the after-effects of years of brutal conflict. It was presented to a high-level meeting on Youth Employment in February 2007 hosted by UNIDO, the African Union, UNDP, the UN Youth Employment Network, the ILO and other agencies in Accra, Ghana by its principal author, Alpha Bacar Barry and other members of the NGO coalition. It was generally well received, but some governments wondered how the sub-regional approach would fit into their existing initiatives. Since then, the glacially slow machinery of governments and the UN have ground out a useful, costed Programme of Action, and – if all goes well – will see some implementation of work on the ground early in 2008.

However, whether or not or how it may be implemented is not the focus of this paper: my purpose is to outline a policy that some government – any LDC government with the courage and faith in its young people that matches my own – will implement.

The urgent need in the MRU region is to create 4.5 million jobs for unemployed youth. It is a considerable challenge, but there is massive potential. It is lush, green and fertile. There are good port facilities for export, and the road systems, though not great, are adequate for commercial transport most of the year. There are great opportunities to grow the internal market for fruit juices, meat, coffee, rice and other staples. I bought packets of pineapple juice imported from Thailand on the streets of Freetown, while pineapples grown in northern Sierra Leone are rotting in the markets of Kambia Town. There are business opportunities in tourism

– especially eco- and adventure-tourism. Youth are well placed to exploit them, if supported and trained to be successful in doing so.

The young people of the Mano River Union Youth Employment Forum believe that this youth-led, adult-supported, co-managed infrastructure has the capacity to do so. I fervently believe so too.

The Three-level Approach

Youth-led Development in the world's Least-developed Countries aims to create jobs for young people at three levels, teaching them skills, improving their social attitudes and raising their self-esteem along the way. The levels are:

1. Youth-led Business Start-ups (YLBS-Us): Basic private sector development. Small investments, $500-$1000 each, to start a small ruminant or horticultural enterprise; a food-processing plant (mango and pineapple juice); bee-keeping initiatives; bakery, brewing, web-design, communications and service provision amongst a myriad of other possibilities. Basic financial services and IT training are also good income-generating vehicles for young people. They generate an income from the internal market, often from direct selling to the customer. As long as proper market research is conducted ahead of implementation, young entrepreneurs who can design their efforts to meet a real – not imagined – need will be successful. The plethora of tailoring, craft, hairdressing, soap-making and tie-dyeing initiatives that today swamp the markets and frustrate youth who fail to move their product, will be avoided.

2. Youth-led Social Enterprise (YLSE): Young people are natural conservers of the environment, eager to plant trees, clean up parks or beaches, and preserve wilderness areas, habitats and wildlife. They are also excellent providers of teaching and basic health-care services. There are the young girls supported by UNICEF and the World Bank in rural Baluchistan, running 'front-room schools' to teach literacy and numeracy to their peers in villages where fathers would not normally allow their daughters to go to a formal schools.[8] Another famous example is of the young Brazilian from São Paulo who set up a care programme for his grandfather because he was old and lonely: the idea caught on, and now hundreds of young people work in teams to care for and entertain elderly relatives.[9] In Germany, care for the elderly is almost totally dependent upon the Zivildienst programme, and most EVS volunteers spend a lot of their time emptying bed-pans.[10] The EVS and Zivildienst programmes are not genuine youth-led social enterprises: the government set them up, so to that extent they exploit young people's goodwill. The Brazilian example is a genuine YLSE because it was led and inspired by young people themselves. They do it because they want to, not because a government, seeking to save money, tells them to.

3. Youth-led public works: Needs assessment in many communities often throws up the need for basic infrastructure – water, sanitation, roads, a bridge, a school building, a health centre. In some countries, young people have been organised to help build these public infrastructures – and, working as volunteers, they do so at a greatly reduced cost. From the youth perspective, such schemes are valuable if, while doing them, they learn skills which make them more attractive to future employers or more able to set up their own businesses later on: a young person who has worked some years on building bridges or water supply schemes is more likely to make a success of a construction company than one who has not. Such programmes also provide experiential learning of project management skills, so that future youth-led companies can bid for future infrastructure contracts put out for tender by government. If such contracts have a certain quota to be assigned to YLD initiatives, infrastructure projects could be an enormous growth area for youth employment without attracting the stigmata of 'slave labour' or 'chain gang' which are identified with the road-building programmes of Hitler or Mao Tse Tung.

A Structure for Nationwide Delivery: ownership by all

The youth who designed this Mano River Union initiative are frustrated by many things. They are sick of development professionals who address a meeting of youth NGOs once a year and call it 'youth participation'. They are fed up with streams of 'researchers' arriving in their air-conditioned land-cruisers to inspect their misery. They want action and investment NOW. Worst, they are sick of 'pet donor initiatives' that deliver great benefits to a few selected villages – helping the few at the expense of the many. They fail to generate the critical mass of activity that can kick-start the

Administrative Infrastructure
for the
Mano River Union Youth Employment Forum

MRU-YEF EXECUTIVE COMMITTEE
Chair-Convenors: Governments of Guinea, Cote D'Ivoire, Liberia & Sierra Leone
Members: Youth leaders; Business Sector representatives; UN agency reps; donor reps; Senior Programme Country managers; Intl. Volunteer reps.

NATIONAL EXECUTIVE COUNCIL x 3
Chair-Convenor: Individual Country Government
Members: Youth Leaders; UN agency reps; donor government reps; senior management & NGOs.

NATIONAL EXECUTIVE COUNCIL x 3
Chair-Convenor: Individual Country Government
Members: Youth Leaders; UN agency reps; donor government reps; senior management & NGOs.

NATIONAL HQ x 3
Adult Management: Intl. + Natl. Project Directors; Intl. + Natl. Finance Directors;
Staff: 30 x Desk Officers: 15 x natl. 15 x Intl. volunteers

NATIONAL HQ x 3
Adult Management: Intl. + Natl. Project Directors; Intl. + Natl. Finance Directors;
Staff: 30 x Desk Officers: 15 x natl. 15 x Intl. volunteers

REGIONAL HUBS x 82
Management: 2 x Directors
Staff: 10 x Desk Officers

REGIONAL HUBS x 82
Management: 2 x Directors
Staff: 10 x Desk Officers

1,000+ Village HUBS 2 x staff

1,000+ Village HUBS 2 x staff

1,000+ Village HUBS 2 x staff

1,000+ Village HUBS 2 x staff

1,000+ Village HUBS 2 x staff

economy of a whole country. That is why they designed a structure to be able to touch "every single young citizen who wants to be part of the solution". Unlike the UN's Peace-Building Commission which is only investing in Sierra Leone, the youth approach reflects the conclusions of every major study of the region – that the security of one country depends on the security of all. The history of the last decades demonstrates that insecurity spills across frontiers. Their regional, cross-border approach is not an option but a structural necessity.

At the top of their organisational pyramid (see facing page) sits the Executive Committee, convened by the ministers of each country under the auspices of the union secretariat. All stakeholders are represented, the youth themselves, the private sector, international donors and as many ministers of the governments that can be persuaded to come along. Trust between youth and government is not very high, so the main goal of the youth representatives is to ensure that they know where every cent being spent in their name has gone. For the government and international donors, the goal is to ensure that youth activity is focussed on achieving the wider development goals of the region – giving them the opportunity to harness the massive energy and skills of their young citizens to help achieve their nation-building goals. The Executive Committee meets once a year at a youth summit to chart progress across the region toward existing goals, and to set new ones.

Each country has a National Executive Council which meets two to three times a year: all three governments have several programmes and ideas for programmes on youth employment. Many international NGOs working in their countries have initiatives underway. The purpose of the National Executive is to coordinate all these: bringing together government, youth groups, international donors and the private sector to ensure that all programmes assist in meeting the goal of reaching every young citizen in their countries with the opportunity for self-improvement through Youth-led Development.

The National Executive includes, and is largely led by, young people. They employ the National Director(s) of the programme, experienced young people with verve and fire to make things work, not bureaucratic government placemen. As much as possible, expatriate technical assistance will be provided by young people – where possible, international volunteers who have already served some years in the country. The National Executive also appoints the Finance Director, who reports to them, so that all youth can see where the money goes.

The national headquarters is set up on the model of the Peace Child White House – a team of international and local volunteers supervised, supported and guided by the National Director(s) to implement the directives of the National Executive Council. They will also be involved in supporting and monitoring projects in the National Capital Area – so they will have hands-on experience of the kind of work being done at the regional and village hubs. That work is to go out and meet with young people wherever they are: in schools, in colleges, hanging around on street corners, meeting in informal groups, in youth councils and youth associations. The job is to find out what their concerns are. If, as is often the case, their chief concern is to find a job and they are willing and eager to do just about anything, the MRU-YEF team invite them to join their task force. The task forces meet in groups of 15-20 at the rented hub office and learn the skills of needs assessment and market research – so that they can work where the gaps are in local, regional and national markets. Clearly this is where the technical assistance and national policy guidance is extremely important – as the pair of volunteers working directly with the young people have to be able to advise and guide them exactly where the needs – and market opportunities – lie beyond the frontiers of the young people's own experience. In this way, the YLBS-Us are collaborations between the rural youth and the MRU-YEF staff volunteers.

The hub office also serves as a business incubator, offering the young entrepreneurs a one-stop shop for business registration, loan agreements, office space, administrative and accounting support and one-on-one mentorship. Each hub is designed with the sole purpose of ensuring that every young person's initiative is successful – or, if any do fail, that skills are learned, and sponsors get full reports explaining the reasons for failure.

YBI and the Prince's Trust have a policy that states that there should be no guidance – no prompting on what kind of business ventures the young people should pursue. They believe, and their experience confirms, that the only way that a young person will fight and struggle to make a YLBS-U a success is if it is entirely their own idea. Our experience is slightly at odds with this: in LDCs and other areas of considerable disadvantage, we find young people almost completely bereft of ideas – too numbed by the daily grind of coping strategies and responsibility for peers and siblings to be able to raise their eyes to any longer-term horizons. Such young people may not be ready for their own YLBS-U but, and YBI and PT agree on this, they may benefit greatly by working on another young person's YLBS-U – and, in time, come to have the confidence and the skills to start their own. It is a nurturing, confidence-building process – and every pair that goes out seeking to support young people is at the sharp end of this process.

Differential Mentorship: three levels of support for the youth

The evidence of the Prince's Trust in relation to mentorship should, we believe, guide the elaboration of YLD policy. Remember: with a good mentor, two out of three youth-led business start-ups are still running and growing after three years. Without the mentor, the success ratio drops to one in five. Mentorship is at the heart of the approach we recommend for youth-led development. Co-management seeks to give young people ownership – genuine ownership, share capital – their name, their credit – for any projects developed in a YLD strategy. In this nationwide strategy that seeks to support and empower young people in every corner of a country to take their future in their hands and make a go of setting up a small business or a social enterprise, we believe that young people need to be supported 24/7 in order to have the very best chance of success. Some youth will not require that support – fine! That leaves the mentors more time for those that do, and some will need a very great deal of support. Sometimes, it will all be in vain as the initiative will fail. But, as the Trust has proved again and again, the education and skills learned by every young person doing a project is such that they then become far more employable to other businesses and much more likely to succeed in their next enterprise.

The challenge for YLD in some LDCs is that appropriate business mentors don't exist (this is why the Prince's Youth Business International has not gone into many of them.) The private sector is so fragile that, sometimes, they see any new business start-up – whether led by youth or anyone else! – as a threat. So, in LDCs, traditional approaches to mentorship don't work. Thus we have developed a system we call 'differential mentorship' – mentorship by both local private sector business people, educated local volunteers and highly trained international volunteers. Together, this team mentorship approach creates the three levels of support which we believe will be at least as good as the single, caring business mentor and in many cases even better, as the two young volunteer members of the team are available 24/7. In addition to the base team, our scheme envisages an oversight team of local and expatriate business development mentors who are on hand to trouble-shoot particular problems, to review business plans and advise on which projects have the best chance of success.

The pair is based at the local village hub, or in neighbourhood hubs in urban areas. They help the young entrepreneurs to develop their business plans, providing business services and training in the early days of the project start-up. Importantly, in the best co-management tradition, the pair keep in touch and consult with the local private sector and community leaders to ensure that whatever the young people plan is supportive of generic business and community development in the area. The support of community leaders – local government officials etc. – provides a third level of mentorship which the young social and commercial entrepreneurs can draw upon.

These three different tiers of differential mentorship provide the young people with a technical assistance support system that has to be set in place across a nation before successful YLD policy can be attempted nationwide.

Key Policy Elements introduced by the Youth

The young people who designed this Nationwide YLD project went further. In their own words, they recommended the inclusion of the following key elements of management infrastructure which would not normally occur in an economic or policy development strategy. To me, these elements reveal all that is wonderful and unique about a genuine youth-led approach to development. So without apology, I quote them in their entirety:[11]

> **Gender Mainstreaming**: For centuries, African women have been oppressed by African men. We know this now. Young people are already changing their attitudes. We are very proud that the first female African Head of State was elected in Liberia – one of our MRU countries. But gender mainstreaming needs to be a consistent element of our YLD policies to ensure that communities across our region honour and give opportunities to young women in exactly the same way as they do to young men. We will play our part by ensuring that 50 percent of projects funded by the MRU-YEF are led by young female project managers, that women in the community are consulted in the course of the needs assessment in the same way as men, and that each project team includes as many young women as young men.
>
> We are very confident that this policy component of YLD will be achieved easily – as all our youth groups are 100 percent committed to the empowerment of

young women. (Indeed, we worry if there will be enough young men eager enough to sign up!) But in rural areas, engrained attitudes take time to change – and we shall be sensitive, but firm, in our insistence on the engagement, full involvement and empowerment of young women in every village hub.

Inclusion of Youth with disabilities: All our groups are intensely aware of the disadvantages suffered by the deaf, the blind and partially sighted, the wheelchair-bound and those suffering other disabilities. They are rejected by their families, sidelined by their communities, who seem just to wish they would disappear. Because of recent wars, there are many young disabled youth in our countries. The MRU-YEF will seek out, empower and work with them. By showing that we care, we hope to inspire them to come up with workable business plans and projects in which they can be centrally involved. Likewise, each project funded will be encouraged to engage young disabled people as a requirement of getting the highest evaluation points. Much research is needed on this area – and we need to collect detailed data for our records. All we are stating here is our determination to do the most we can to make disabled young people know that YLD is for them.

A Comprehensive Regional Communication Plan: A big obstacle to
cross-border collaboration of any kind in the MRU is the absence of region-wide media. Youth have raised this problem before. In 2000, the MRU Youth Parliament called for the creation of a region-wide youth newspaper in French and English. For a successful, region-wide YLD programme, such a newspaper is not just a nice thing to do: it is the essential communication tool to ensure that targets are being set and recorded, resources are used effectively, good practice is shared, the lessons of others' mistakes are learned, whistles are blown on corruption – and that the reaching of targets is appropriately praised.

We plan to set up a website, a TV station and a radio station. Each medium is important, especially for funders keen to monitor the expenditure of their funds. But not every town, not every village has access to such technologies. Newspapers get everywhere – and they can be stored in offices to allow those developing business plans to look back over stories that may guide and inspire them.

Develop Youth-friendly Financial Services: The absence of banks or
any kind of financial services outside the capitals of our countries is an enormous obstacle to the development of business or social enterprise. It means that

we have all grown up with no knowledge of mortgages, bank loans or even bank accounts. Financial literacy is an essential pre-condition of successful entrepreneurs. One of the things that we hope our international teams of young volunteers and mentors will help us with is to help them to set up simple mobile banking services and teach young project managers financial literacy. For too long our businesses have suffered from the need to carry money round in suitcases. Modern, electronic financial services must be a priority for the YLD networks we are setting up. We need to research other models to try to replicate 'what works' in our countries. One of the models that appeals to us is the Credit Agricole of France – which started out by making loans for young farmers in rural areas. But even if it were in place, adults keep telling us that young people are 'viewed as a high credit risk'. That may well be the 'view', but as in our experience no bank has ever extended a loan to a young person, we wonder upon what objective evidence that 'view' is based? Our Plan for Action seeks to test the hypothesis that, like the women borrowers who helped launch the Grameen Bank, young people, properly mentored, can be an extremely low credit risk for lenders.

Caravan of Ex-Combatants and AIDS Orphans: The achievements of young project managers who come from backgrounds of considerable disadvantage – as ex-combatants, orphans, and those living with HIV-AIDS – need to be shared with those who may be suffering for similar reasons. In 2001, 35 Guinean and 15 Sierra Leonean young people from these backgrounds organised a caravan that travelled through all three countries, speaking to schools, informal gatherings of young people and youth associations, alerting them to the horror of war and the vigilance needed to preserve the peace. We want to organise a similar kind of caravan every year as a way of promoting peace, understanding and the MRU-YEF programme. We believe that this will inspire many young people to recognise their own ability to start a project or a business. Each year it will travel a different route for six weeks visiting war-afflicted communities where there is a need to boost creativity in the business plans being submitted.

Travelling Trade fair: Either alongside, or separate from, the Ex-combatants caravan, we propose a travelling trade fair to inspire and develop markets for our goods. For the first couple of years it will be subsidised. After that, it will be financed by the advertising budgets of new business start-ups. Its sole purpose is to generate sales and achieve greater market share for YLD products as well as, like the Caravan, to inspire and attract new young entrepreneurs.

Youth Commission on Good Governance: The MRU-YEF requires a youth-led commission to improve the conduct of government in our countries. Though we all know some excellent government officers, we have all encountered much corruption, incompetence and laziness. We are sick of it and are afraid that we will descend into such sleaze ourselves unless we take active steps to stop ourselves. This Commission is not about pointing fingers, or duplicating the work of Anti-Corruption Departments. Rather, we seek to engrain the habits of good governance in our generation – transparency, efficiency and an attitude that will not tolerate corruption. Also we want to promote procedures that require the minimum of signatures and paperwork. The Commission will offer daily seminars on good governance run by the young staff of the MRU-YEF. All seminars will be open and free to all. Students of political science and government officers, young and old, will be especially welcome.

Annual Summit on YLD: This will be an annual assessment of progress made, problems that have arisen, and solutions applied. The outcome will be an annually updated, co-owned Youth Employment Strategy. We shall ask our youth ministers to convene and chair this annual summit to bring together the youth leaders of the MRU-YEF with other ministers (labour, finance, industry) who should have an interest in the scheme.

Promoting the Voluntary Service Ethic: Our programme seeks young educated people to give a year of service in return for accommodation and meals at each of the MRU-YEF national, regional or village hubs. It will be a fun year, with volunteers working in each other's countries, getting to know the differences and the similarities. Our young people will work alongside the international volunteers, introducing them to African culture and history, while learning many employable skills (IT etc.) from them, and at the same time making new friends and being a part of our region-building, job-creating, peace-building success story.

National Network of Job Centres and Business Incubators: Our plan provides for the setting up of YMCA-style Hostels/business development Hubs across the Mano River Union. The international volunteers will live and work there, providing IT training, business plan development assistance, project management support and general mentoring. Peace Child International has pioneered the development of such a centre with its White House headquarters in Britain and its partner centre in Bangalore, India. These are models we want to replicate across our three countries. Land has already been acquired for one in Guinea, and negotiations are under way to find land for national HQs in the other two countries. District and village hubs will be rented houses working on the same model. Each hub will offer young people all the advice and training they need to start and run a YLBS-U or social enterprise. The hubs will also allow young people to submit their CVs to the job-seeker website, where employers can match the skills of individual youth to the jobs they need to fill.

Clean up the Informal Sector: Our plan intends to use these centres to help young street-sellers and other youth suffering in the informal sector. We have no great wish to suffer the bureaucratic procedures of registration or pay taxes, but it has to be better than being at the mercy of unscrupulous operators selling car phone chargers, paper tissues and videos on the street 12 hours a day. Our centres will give these energetic, streetwise youth the chance to review their markets, develop a proper business plan and move into the formal sector. We fully expect to find the best business plans for the YLBS-Us, and some of the best volunteers and peer educators, from this sector.

Develop Cross-Border Services: Many of us nurture the hope that the African Union will become a union of the African nations, just as the European Union is union of European nations. African governments are clearly not ready to embrace such a vision, but the youth are. We are supporting the MRU-YEF so that we can develop a cross-border customs union, freely trading agricultural produce, manufactured goods, energy and water supply. In all the programmes we undertake, we shall look for the cross-border, MRU-angle which will allow us to learn each other's languages, share each other's cultures, and become closer as a union of peoples.

Initiate Inter-University Exchange Schemes: European students enjoy enormous benefits from Erasmus, Comenius and Leonardo exchange programmes. No such programmes exist for students in our region. The MRU-YEF will launch formal university exchanges as part of the process of building regional cohesion: students and staff from our region's universities will be encouraged to spend a year or a semester in another country. In this way, we shall build intellectual capital across the region.

Regional Citizenship Training: The Youth Good Governance Commission will promote a region-wide programme of seminars, workshops, cabarets and other presentations to draw young people's attention to their civic responsibilities to promote human rights, resist corruption, promote the rule of law and adhere to the highest standards of democracy. Run by young people from different countries, this programme will embed a culture of good citizenship across the region.

Comprehensive programme of Literacy, IT & Sustainability training: Bridging the digital divide is a key goal of this programme. The international volunteers will be encouraged to bring a laptop to donate to their village or regional hub. Through contacts in Europe and North America, every effort will be made to bring in decent computers for schools, internet-capable computers of recent vintage, not the clapped-out cast-offs peddled by some international computer recycling companies. We will work with technology partners to get high-speed internet connections and, in all our programmes, work with the young people so that they can experience the value and assistance that modern IT systems deliver. Youth are growing up with computers. Computer literacy is second nature to them, so everything, from the preparation of the proposal, the calculation of budgets, schedules, the preparation of reports will be done on computer. Each centre will run IT courses for young people – charging small course fees to keep out time-wasters.

In addition, literacy and numeracy courses will be provided through the social enterprise strand of this initiative. The young peer educators will also be trained to deliver modules on sustainable lifestyles, using games, experiential learning, debates, hot-seat improvisations and other fun teaching methods to cover such subjects as: environmental conservation; healthy lifestyles (including personal hygiene, nutrition, sexual health and HIV-AIDS awareness); waste management (recycling, composting etc.); travel and consumption habits; energy and renewables and other sustainability issues.

In a nutshell, the MRU-YEF approach to YLD is all about setting up professional, profitable businesses, supported by well-managed, effective social support structures. The businesses must be registered, and pay taxes and decent salaries for decent work. Their working conditions will be regulated to be safe and worker-friendly. Because they are youth-led they are frequently more fun, more dynamic, and more creative than elder-led businesses. And they can certainly be more profitable because, properly trained, motivated and supported by local business, community, plus local youth and international volunteer mentors, they will be successful. Failure is not an option in the ethic of YLD: "100 percent success rate is the target – and we shall not rest until we achieve it."

The next YLD challenge is to harness the energy and talent of the local volunteer mentors so that, when they return from their year of working with disadvantaged rural and urban youth, they can use what they have learned to start and run the larger SMEs that will provide employment to hundreds, eventually thousands of their generation and consolidate the economies of their currently fragile countries. They require a whole new level of business incubator support and technical assistance which will, we hope, grow organically from the YLD model described here. Governments and donors should be considering, and planning for, this next challenge as they invest in this entry-level scheme.

Many development professionals point out that these benefits have been known about and pursued for many years. It is well known that Ghanaian farmers can produce excellent cotton at prices far lower than the US sub-sidised industry. Sugar is another market where LDCs could build leading positions, were it not for the culture of subsidies in the industrialised North – this $352-billion dollar wall against building prosperity in the world's least-developed countries. The problem has been known about and dis-cussed in European capitals for decades. News footage of tractors and muck-spreaders on the Champs Elysées are testament to how firmly the battle lines are drawn, and how fiercely they are defended.

YLD has no quick fix to this – perhaps the central obstacle to enabling LDCs to 'trade' rather than 'aid' their way out of poverty. However, in the long term expanding numbers of returning European and North American volunteers, with the injustice of the subsidy regimes in their home countries burning in their ears, may be able to effect change. There is considerable sup-port already in some countries for change: powerful interest groups in Europe and North America have been defeated on some occasions. YLD volunteers, properly informed and organised, might be able to provide some glue to knit together the coalitions necessary to overthrow what is arguably the greatest obstacle to making poverty history in our lifetimes.

That would be the ultimate victory for YLD: opening up the gates to export markets for the YLBS-Us to extend remarkable, sustainable prosper-ity across the poorest parts of the world over the next decades. It is a long-term process, but there is a brave new world out there waiting to be discovered. Mortality dictates that today's young people will one day inherit the world we live in today: logic and common sense dictates that today's elder statesmen should move quickly to implement the kind of nationwide YLD programmes the young people have themselves designed to address, not just the challenge of youth unemployment but also the wider challenges of preserving the peace, combating corruption and – centrally – growing the economy while at the same time conserving the environmental resource base on which all economic activity depends.

I trust that some of you, reading this, will be persuaded to empower and enable young people to rise to the towering challenges that face them in their lifetimes by supporting the kinds of programmes that work can usefully be gathered under the heading Youth-led Development.

"I would like to offer my remarks today particularly to the young people of the Middle East – and of the world. Last week, in Paris, I met with youth leaders who represented organisations with more than 120 million members worldwide. The meeting also included rural youth and street kids; children orphaned by AIDS and civil conflict; Roma youth and youth with disabilities. They met in peace and with mutual respect. They asked why our generation could not do the same. They said: "We are ready to be part of the solution, to be partners." But, they also said, "We do not want a future based only economic considerations – there must be something more." They challenged us about values and beliefs. My colleagues and I were inspired by their passion and idealism. Soon, young people will start working in the Bank's country offices, to help review projects and suggest initiatives. We will also ask governments to enable youth to participate in discussions of poverty reduction strategies. Mr. Chairman: by the year 2015, there will be 3 billion people under the age of 25. They are the future. But, as the young people in Paris said most forcibly, they are also the now." – **James D. Wolfensohn to the Board of Governors, World Bank Group, Dubai, Sept. 2003**

Afterword

"Our gravest threat on the planet remains the threat of massive war. My worry is that we are gambling recklessly with a '2014' to match the year 1914. Nearly one hundred years ago, in 1914, the peace was sundered by the Guns of August, and the 20th century never quite recovered. World War I almost literally came out of nowhere. A happy march of soldiers to win each nation's honour within a few weeks turned into four years of mass carnage, the Bolshevik Revolution, the rise of Hitler, the Holocaust, and more. Our war in Iraq, our threats to Iran, and even the growing anti-Chinese sentiments in the US Senate – all raise the stakes of a similar disaster on our generation's watch." – **Jeffery Sachs, 2007 BBC Reith Lectures**[1]

Lord Ashdown, the UN's chief of the peace-keeping forces in Bosnia, was also bleakly pessimistic in a recent interview saying that, "If we think that the era of big wars is over, we may be gravely mistaken."[2] Tony Blair came to power 10 years ago celebrating, with some satisfaction that his was "the first European generation to have lived their lives without having to go to war." Yet he went on to fight six of them!

For the youth of today, facing the multiple threats of global warming, population growth, resource depletion and cultural intolerance, entertaining the possibility of big wars is a thought too chilling to contemplate. They feel, correctly, that the world simply does not have the time or the resources to expend on such insanities – either human or material! Throughout his Reith lecture, Sachs rails against the Bush administration's bloated military budget of $623 billion – while only spending $4.5 billion on Africa and, under pressure from the Christian right, practically nothing on programmes that would allow people in developing countries to limit their family size.

Rarely, if ever, has a US administration been on the wrong side of history on so many issues as the current one. A bumper sticker seen frequently in

Washington DC states simply: "December 31st 2008 – the End of an Error". We have to hope that the subsequent administration will move quickly to correct the errors of the Bush one and give global leadership on the global challenges we face. Reaching back to the great American success stories of civilian service – starting with Roosevelt's Civilian Conservation Corps, on through the Peace Corps, VISTA and Clinton's Americorps – we need the United States of America to give a lead on the most compelling argument of all for YLD.

Global Security

It is a truism, fondly stated by all lovers of science fiction, that the only sure way for the peoples of the world to collaborate is as the result of invasion by another planet. The War of the Worlds! The generation of young people currently growing up faces a *de facto* war for the world, in the form of global climate change, mass poverty, water shortages, deforestation etc. How they deal with it, in the face of mounting inter-religious, international and inter-cultural tension, is perhaps the greatest challenge they face. "Trust builds trust, cooperation begets cooperation," says Jeffrey Sachs, suggesting how that philosophy can lead to peace and mid-century prosperity. The other route, he warns, causes "cooperation to collapse – and a 2014 repeat of 1914." Recalling John Kennedy's great speech of June 1963, he reminds us that "we would all get caught up in a dangerous cycle where suspicion breeds suspicion and new weapons beget counter-weapons and we devote to weapons massive sums of money that could be better devoted to combating ignorance, poverty and disease."[3]

That is the disaster which must be avoided. In my final claim for the extraordinary benefits of YLD, I would argue that getting squadrons of young people – Chinese, American, Iraqis, Europeans, North Africans, Iranians, Pakistanis, Indians and Latin Americans – all working together with the young people of the world's Least Developed Countries, fighting together the only war worth fighting – against poverty, climate change and equity in the post-carbon world – will create a world of global co-operation the like of which has never been seen.

The other massive challenge faced by today's youth is planning and building new infrastructure for the world they will be living in by the time they reach their fifties and sixties: a world with no more, or much-reduced, fossil fuel resources. Planning for a post-carbon, solar hydrogen economy requires that the world comes together, and supports its poorest members, in a way they never needed before. And the opportunities in the hotter countries of Africa are immense: they could become the generators of hydrogen and supplier of the world's energy resources in ways barely imagined by current economists. That is at the heart of YLD's challenge for the future – and young people from across the world express themselves ready to work together to address it.

Ideas for a World Development Corps have been floating around for some years. President Eisenhower was one of the first to give flesh and bones to the idea with his 'People-to-People' initiative – and it was perhaps a considerable sadness to him, as well to other internationalists of the time, that the US Peace Corps was set up as an initiative open exclusively to Americans – a mistake which means it still gets perceived by many as a neo-colonial extension of US foreign policy.

A group called World Corps [4] was set up in Seattle, and still operates in Kenya, India and the Philippines. An idea for a European Voluntary Humanitarian Assistance Corps (EVHAC) was included in the ill-fated European Constitution.[5] It is now the time to shake the dust off these old ideas, and plan and budget for their immediate implementation. For, however much they can help the youth of the LDCs (and I hope I have proved in this paper that they can help a lot!), getting Muslim and Western youth working alongside each other to support young Africans start and succeed in small YLD businesses, will bring these young, potential adversaries together in a way that no other educational or exchange exercise ever could.

And by being together in that idealistic, service environment, volunteering their time, energy and skill, they will learn about the absolute priorities for our planet. Firstly the moral priorities of caring for the sick, the elderly, those without hope, the hungry, the destitute and those oppressed by human rights abuse or cultural discrimination. Secondly, they will learn about the imperative of addressing the post-carbon future; the need to secure water supplies, effective sanitation, wage the attitudinal fight against HIV-AIDS, link the world across all remaining digital divides. And, while they are working together, they will learn to combat the unfair subsidy regimes that, more than any other single issue, condemn their peers in the LDCs to lives of grinding poverty. Finally, their prejudices and preconceptions about each other will melt away as they have done for years in all exchange programmes as the natural willingness of young people to be affectionate and have a good time spills over the encrusted remnants of fear and inherited dislike. Many credit the Franco-German youth exchange schemes developed after World War Two with preparing the ground for their bilateral relationship which forms the beating heart of the European Union. I firmly believe that the kinds of friendships forged in the hothouse atmosphere of our US-Soviet exchanges the 1980s – friendships which last until this day, in some cases – provide a human foundation for peace which will survive any risk of re-starting the Cold War mentalities.

The details and the costs of this World Corps idea are not hard to figure out. They would cost a small fraction of the increased development assistance currently planned – and an even tinier fraction of our trillion dollar+ defence budgets. And they would deliver vastly increased global security while at the same time making poverty history! For if we insist, as I suggest, that 50 percent of all initiatives are income-generating small businesses, this will create the middle-class, tax-paying business base essential to grow the economies of the LDCs. At the same time, the social enterprises will ensure the schools, the training schemes, the hospitals and care systems for the elderly, the disabled, the orphans and the mentally ill are firmly in place. They will support these societies to become caring democracies – supportive of rights-based approaches, with strong civil societies which insist on good governance and transparency from their leaders.

It will be a bumpy road, of course, but investing in the security of cooperation, trust and friendship between members of the rising generation has to be a better use of funding than the mediaeval approach that uses only armies and military hardware. We have just watched the USA spend $600 billion dollars trying – and signally failing – to bring peace, prosperity and democracy to Iraq. How much better would it have been to bring Sunni and Shia Iraqi students to work together in an international team of volunteers in Africa, learning about their role as part of the global family. Inclusion and dialogue is, as the UN has found, always better than exclusion and aggression.

Jeffrey Sachs quoted the famous lines from John F. Kennedy's June 1963 speech:[6]

> "For in the final analysis, our most basic common link is that we all inhabit this small planet. We all breathe the same air. We all cherish our children's future. And we are all mortal."

David Gordon used the same words in "Please Listen to me!"[7] – a key song from Peace Child. Another of his songs is based on Martin Luther King's "I have a dream" speech:

"I have a dream that one day this nation will rise up and live out the true meaning of its creed: 'We hold these truths to be self-evident, that all men are created equal.'

"I have a dream that one day on the red hills of Georgia, the sons of former slaves and the sons of former slave owners will be able to sit down together at the table of brotherhood. I have a dream that my four little children will one day live in a nation where they will not be judged by the color of their skin but by the content of their character."[8]

Along with Mahatma Gandhi's dictum "my life is my message"[9] and Abraham Lincoln's observation that "the best way to destroy your enemy is to make him your friend",[10] these are the guiding philosophies that point toward a peaceful, sustainable future. They are the messages that must fire the hearts and minds of all young YLD volunteers.

It would be Pollyanna-ish to think that years ahead will be 100 percent conflict-free. It would be even more foolish to believe that those conflicts can be resolved by traditional military means. (Unless, of course, one seeks to create a world of gated communities of the rich fighting off the intrusive masses of the poor and the dispossessed.)

Youth-led Development provides an approach to global security which engenders ever-closer bonds between the rising generation of the human family. That kind of security, which saves and nurtures lives, is priceless! But, as we have seen, the price through YLD is significantly lower than any approach involving just military measures.

"Man is small, and, therefore, small is beautiful. People living in the poorest parts of the world have a know-how that we don't have. They are survival artists, and it is quite certain that if there should be a real resources crisis, a real ecological crisis, these people will survive. Whether you or I will survive is much more doubtful. India will survive, though whether Bombay will survive is more doubtful. That New York will survive is an impossibility. The modern private enterprise system ingeniously employs the human urges of greed and envy as its motive power, but can such a system conceivably deal with the problems we are now having to face? The answer is self-evident: greed and envy demand continuous and limitless economic growth of a material kind, without proper regard for conservation. This type of growth cannot possibly fit into a finite environment." – **E. F. Schumacher**

Appendix I

References and Bibliography

Executive Summary

1. Introduction by Paul Wolfowitz to the 2007 World Development Report; www.worldbank.org/wdr2007
2. Confucius, 450BC: "Tell me, and I will forget; Show me, and I may remember; Involve me, and I will understand." John Dewey, 1938 – "Experience and Education"; David Kolb, Ted Wragg, David Orr et al. This remark was made by Ted Wragg in the presence of the author in September 2004 at a DEA meeting.
3. See: www.unfpa.org/swp/2007/youth/english/story/introduction.html
4. Remarks made by Asif Hasnain, UNIDO at the Accra Conference on Youth Employment, Feb. '07; quoted in the Meeting Report, April 2007; www.unido.org/doc/61678
5. See: www.peacechild.org – click on Be the Change; click on projects;
6. Guardian, "Gap Year Popularity Soars" – http://education.guardian.co.uk/students/story/0,,551291,00
7. Reference: "Co-management – becoming equal partners" – European Commission, April 2006 (David Woollcombe – Project Coordinator) www.co-management.info
8. See: www.aidharmonization.org/secondary-pages/Paris2005 or www.oecd.org/document/18/0, 2340,en_2649_3236398_35401554_1_1_1_1,00.html
9. See: www.whitehouse.gov/omb/budget/fy2006/state.html
20. Lecture: Education as if the Earth Mattered by David Orr; quoted in 'In Context' Magazine, (editor: Robert Gilman) Number 26.

Chapter One: What is Youth-led Development?

1. See: www.princes-trust.org.uk/Main%20Site%20v2/14-30%20and%20need%20help/start%20up%20in%20business/paula%20vika%20hair%20design.asp
2. See: www.princes-trust.org.uk/
3. Explained by Andrew Fiddaman, Deputy Director, YBI in an interview with the author; (12/7/07)
4. Explained by Andrew Fiddaman, Deputy Director, YBI in an interview with the author; (12/7/07)
5. Quote from Jonathan Dimbleby's *The Prince of Wales: a Biography* (Little Brown, 1994. p.364)
6. E-mail from Sarah Henderson, the Prince's Trust of 24/5/07 to the author,
7. YBI Young Entrepreneur of the Year Award Pamphlet;
8. Remark made in an interview with the author, October 2006;
9. Briefing Paper prepared by the YEN West Africa Office, Jan 2007; See:

www.unido.org/doc/61678

10. Casablanca Declaration, August 2003; See: www.peacechild.org – click on WYC Series; read more Morocco – then click to download the complete Declaration. Quote under Finance, Page 9;

11. Martin Meredith quotes Mandela's speech of February 1995 to parliament in his book, State of Africa: "The government literally does not have the money to meet the demands being advanced. Mass action of any kind will not create the resources that the government does not have. We must rid ourselves of the culture of entitlement that leads to the expectation that the government must promptly deliver whatever it is we demand."

12. One example: Keith Urbahn writing in the Yale Daily News: "The problem is that an entitlement culture denies individual responsibility and creates handy excuses for failure. Obese people and smokers claim entitlements to financial compensation by McDonald's and Philip Morris for damage caused by personal indiscretion." www.yaledailynews.com/articles/view/13693?badlink=1

13. See: www.peacechild.org – click on Be the Change! Then – click on projects: these are some examples of the 3,000+ project proposals we have received from such groups over the last five years.

14. See: GTZ youth page: www.gtz.de/en/themen/uebergreifende-themen/jugend/899.htm
Danida – Children and Young People in Danish Development Cooperation – Guidelines
www.ambaccra.um.dk/NR/rdonlyres/72A0A52D-9940-4E50-9889-C94357DFC1D1/0/
ChildrenAndYoungPeopleInDanishDevelopmentCooperation.pdf
Norway: "Three Billion Reasons" –
www.regjeringen.no/en/dep/ud/Documents/Reports-programmes-of-action-and-plans/Reports/2005/Three-billion-reasons.html?id=420398

15. See: www.peacechild.org – click on Be the Change then "Civicus Review"

16. Quote from Jonathan Dimbleby's "The Prince of Wales – a Biography"(Little Brown, 1994 – P. 238)

17. Quote from Don Richardson, Peace Child – Readers Digest, 1981.

18. See: www.unhabitat.org/

19. See: www.icsc.ca/latest/un-habitat-to-set-up-youth-fund.html & Press Release (22 ibid.)

20. Statement to the Closing Ceremony of the UN-Habitat Governing Council, April 2007; see:
www.unhabitat.org/content.asp?cid=4726&catid=14&typeid=8&subMenuId=0

21. Statement by Ms. Mernosh Tajhizadeh, ENJEU; see:
http://hq.unhabitat.org/cdrom/opclose/23_mt.html

22. See: www.unhabitat.org/content.asp?cid=4727&catid=298&typeid=6&subMenuId=0

23. The UK 2001 Census, supported by research from the Joseph Rowntree foundation; the figure is widely quoted by the BBC, MPs and members of the House of Lords, Barnardos and others.

24. Agenda 21, Chapter 25, UN, 1992; see:
www.un.org/esa/sustdev/documents/agenda21/index.htm

Chapter Two: YLD: The Irresistible Proposition

1. See: www.whitehouse.gov/omb/budget/fy2006/state.html
2. Correspondence between the author and young activists about this paper;
3. See: See: www.unfpa.org/swp/2007/youth/english/story/introduction.html
4. Issues in World Health, Johns Hopkins University, supported by USAID; "Can we avoid catastrophe?" www.infoforhealth.org/pr/l12/l12creds.shtml – click on 'Youth at the Centre'; also see: www.youthaidscoalition.org/faq.html – the UN-supported Global Youth Coalition against AIDS;
5. A slide in the presentation by David Orr at the Be the Change Conference, London May 2006; see: https://bethechange.org.uk/dvd.cfm
6. Surveys carried out by this author and other members of the Peace Child Intl. team in Argentina, India, Uganda, Kenya, Morocco, Sierra Leone, Guinea, Chile, Mexico and elsewhere in the last 2 years.
7. Briefing Paper prepared by the YEN West Africa Office, Jan 2007; See: www.unido.org/doc/61678
8. ILO Global Employment Trends for Youth 2006: www.ilo.org/public/english/employment/strat/ global06.htm
9. ILO Global Employment Trends for Youth 2006: ibid.
10. ILO Global Employment Trends for Youth 2006: ibid.
11. New York Times – Farm Subsidies That Kill By Nicholas D. Kristof; Friday, 5 July, 2002; it is the figure quoted at the Johannesburg World Summit for Sustainable Development by several speakers, including the author of a planet: "Killing the World with Public Funds."
12. Explained by Andrew Fiddaman, Deputy Director, YBI in an interview with the author; (12/7/07)
13. UNDP Human Development Report 2006 – table 18
14. UNDP Human Development Report 2006 – table 18
15. The Millennium Project Report – 'Investing in Development'; see: www.unmillenni-umproject. org/press/prelease_eng.htm
16. P J O'Rourke, 'Eat the Rich' (Picador 1998) – Chapter 8 'How to make nothing from everything'
17. Paris Decl. See: www.oecd.org/document/18/0, 2340,en_2649_3236398_35401554_1_1_1_1,00.html
18. See: www.epwp.gov.za
19. Interview of Judy Olsen, Deputy Director, US Peace Corps with the author
20. John F. Kennedy's Inaugural Address, Friday January 20, 1961; see: www.bartleby. com/124/pres56.html
21. The dominant feature of personal interviews with members of the UK Youth Parliament at the International Development Meeting, UKYP, Leicester, July 2006

Chapter Three: The Evidence of Success

1. 2007 World Development Report, Development & the next generation (p. 208 & 13 other times)
2. http://topics.developmentgateway.org/youth/rc/ItemDetail.do~1036524?intcmp=700

3. http://topics.developmentgateway.org/youth/rc/ItemDetail.do~1037794?intcmp=700
4. http://topics.developmentgateway.org/youth/rc/ItemDetail.do~1057271?intcmp=700
5. See: www.youthactionnet.org
6. Our Time is Now (Pearson Foundation: 2005) Page 4
7. Our Time is Now (Pearson Foundation: 2005) Page 9
8. Our Time is Now (Pearson Foundation: 2005) Page 13 – following;
9. Ashoka Youth Venture – www.ashoka.org/youthventure
10. See: www.ashoka.org/views/video?filter0=164 – to view the video this quotes from;
11. See: www.ashoka.org
12. "Leading Social Entrepreneurs" (Ashoka – 2006) – Page 33
13. See: www.peacechild.org – click on Be the Change
14. See: www.peacechild.org – click on Be the Change – then click on Projects
15. See: www.unido.org/
16. See: Report of High-level Consultation on Youth Employment, Accra, Ghana, February 2007
17. See: Introduction to the MRU Youth Employment Forum document, February 2007
19. See: www.iadb.org/exr/spe/youth/
20. See: www.untechoparamipais.org/
21. See: www.aiesec.org/
22. See: www.aiesec.org/about/our_identity/
23. See: www.freethechildren.com/
24. See: www.kenyaproject.org.uk/
25. For a clear definition of Action Research, see: www.uwe.ac.uk/solar/Principles.htm

Chapter Four: The Imperative of Service

1. See: http://sensoryoverload.typepad.com/sensory_overload/2005/01/shirley_chishol.html
2. Don Eberly & Reuven Gal, "Service without Guns" (2006 – ISBN231571)
3. See the History of War on Want: www.waronwant.org/?lid=1345
4. Don Eberly & Reuven Gal, "Service without Guns" (2006 – ISBN231571)
5. For more details on the brilliant Intl. Baccalaureate programme, see: www.ibo.org/
6. Don Eberly & Reuven Gal, "Service without Guns" (2006 – ISBN231571)
7. Don Eberly & Reuven Gal, "Service without Guns" (2006 – ISBN231571)
8. Exhibits in Museums of the Revolution in Havana, Trinidad and Santa Clara, Cuba
9. See: unesdoc.unesco.org/images/0014/001460/146007e.pdf for the full history of this extraordinary success story of the Sandinista regime.
10. Don Eberly & Reuven Gal, "Service without Guns" (2006 – ISBN231571)
11. Best introduction to this extraordinary story can be found at: www.threegorgesprobe.org/tgp/index.cfm?DSP=content&ContentID=13804
12. Interviews by the author with youth in Hungary, Slovakia, Moldova and Russia (2005-07)
13. See: www.zivildienst.de/ – alles in Deutsch!
14. Don Eberly & Reuven Gal, "Service without Guns" (2006 – ISBN231571)
15. See: www.vso.org.uk/about/cprofiles/eritrea_sandy.asp

Chapter Five: Co-Management: Sharing Responsibility

1. Sign on the desk of Richard Hauser, co-founder with Hepzibah Menuhin of the Centre for Human Rights and Responsibilities, London; noted by his assistant, Eirwen Harbottle;

2. John Stuart Mill, On Liberty (Modern Library Classics, 2004) Page 84;

3. See the UN Resolutions about IYY at : www.un.org/documents/ga/res/36/a36r028.htm

4. Visit the UN website, Youth at the United Nations, which leads to the WPAY and other documents at: www.un.org/esa/socdev/unyin/ga60.htm

5. Stewart Dakers, writing in Society Guardian, 24th July 2007 (page 6)

6. See: www.thecommonwealth.org/subhomepage/152816/

7. See: www.coe.int/youth/

8. Erasmus programme – celebrating 20 years: 1987-2007: http://ec.europa.eu/education/index_en.html

9. Taking Part – Pamphlet by Roger Hart for the Innocenti Institute, 1990, UNICEF; Page 9

10. The Role of Children in Governance – David Woollcombe, University of Durham, 1998;

11. For an introduction to Co-management, see: www.co-management.info/index.php?id=coman00

12. See: www.co-management.info/index.php?id=partner2. It doesn't go deeply into the projects; these were covered in the 1st draft, which can be requested from the author at: david@peacechild.org

Chapter Six: A Policy Framework for a Nationwide YLD Project

1. See: 2007 World Development Report; www.worldbank.org/wdr2007

2. See: www.ambaccra.um.dk/.../0/ChildrenAndYoungPeopleInDanishDevelopment Cooperation.pdf

3. See: www.regjeringen.no/upload/kilde/ud/pla/2005/0005/ddd/pdfv/247957-young.pdf

4. See: www.gtz.de/en/themen/uebergreifende-themen/jugend/899.htm

5. See:http://web.worldbank.org/WBSITE/EXTERNAL/TOPICS/EXTCY/0,,menuPK:396453~page PK:149018~piPK:149093~theSitePK:396445,00.html

6. See: 2007 World Development Report; www.worldbank.org/wdr2007

7. See: www.peacechild.org – click on Be the Change – then click on MRU-YEF;

8. Explained by Steven Umemoto, former Director UNICEF Pakistan, in an interview with the author

9. Presentation at The Geneva Youth of the World Conference, August 1998

10. Reports of EVS Volunteers returning from UK EVS training programmes: they report that almost all the other volunteers they met are working in old people's homes. We have tried to seek independent confirmation of this from the European Commission – without success; but, informally, staff at EVS sending agencies have confirmed that this is true.

11. See: www.peacechild.org – click on Be the Change – then click on MRU-YEF

Afterword

1. You can listen to the lecture or read a transcript at: www.bbc.co.uk/radio4/reith/
2. Remarks made by Lord Ashdown on "Any Questions" – BBC Radio 4, Saturday April 16, 2007
3. You can watch the speech or read it at: www.americanrhetoric.com/speeches/jfkamericanuniversityaddress.html
4. See: www.worldcorps.org/
5. Treaty Establishing A Constitution For Europe Section 3, Humanitarian Aid, Article Iii-223.5; See: http://european-convention.eu.int/docs/Treaty/cv00850.en03.pdf
6. www.americanrhetoric.com/speeches/jfkamericanuniversityaddress.html
7. See: www.peacechild.org – click on History – then click on songs;
8. You can watch the speech or read it at: www.americanrhetoric.com/speeches/mlki-haveadream.htm
9. This is the inscription on the Gandhi monument on Massachusetts Avenue and P Street NW, in Washington DC. The source is not indicated.
10. See: www.quotesforall.com/l/lincolnabraham.htm; that's the famous Lincoln quote – but I first heard the idea from a young Croatian interning at Peace Child who had never heard it. I like the way she said it better: "You cannot destroy your enemy by shooting him; that only makes more enemies. The only sure way to destroy your enemy is by making him your friend." Daniela Zunec, 1991

Appendix II

Organisations and Links

Ashoka / Youth Ventures www.genv.net / www.ashoka.org
Be the Change – Peace Child International www.peacechild.org
Canada World Youth www.cwy-jcm.org
Commonwealth Youth Programme www.thecommonwealth.org/CYP
Commonwealth Youth Exchange Council www.cyec.org.uk
Community Service Volunteers www.csv.org.uk
Council of Europe Youth Centre www.coe.int/youth
Envie d'Agir www.enviedagir.fr (French only)
European Commission Youth dept. www.salto-youth.net/
    ec.europa.eu/youth/program/index_en.html
European Youth Forum   www.youthforum.org
European Youth Foundation galadriel.coe.int/fej/portal/media-type/html/
    country/null/user/anon/page/default.psml?js_language=en
EVS ec.europa.eu/youth/program/sos/vh_evs_en.html

Environmental Youth Alliance www.eya.ca
Fredskorpset www.fredskorpset.no
Free the Children www.freethechildren.com
Global Village Project / United Games www.globalvillageproject.net/
    www.unitedgames.org
Global Youth Action Network www.youthlink.org
Global Youth Service Day www.gysd.net
Hand in Hand www.hihseed.org
International Youth Foundation www.iyfnet.org
ImagineNations www.imaginenations.org
Kenya Education Partnerships www.kenyaproject.org.uk
Norwegian People's Aid www.npaid.org
Nordic Council www.norden.org/unr/uk/index.asp?lang=6
Oxfam International Youth Partnerships www.iyp.oxfam.org
Plan International www.plan-international.org
Post-Carbon Institute www.postcarbon.org
Prince's Trust www.princes-trust.org.uk
Raleigh International www.raleigh.org.uk
Schumacher Society www.schumacher.org.uk
Student Partnership worldwide www.spw.org
Taking IT Global www.takingitglobal.org
Tourism Concern www.tourismconcern.org.uk
Trickle-up www.trickleup.org
UN HABITAT Youth Fund www.unhabitat.org
UNESCO Youth Activities www.unesco.org/youth
UNEP – TUNZA www.unep.org/tunza/youth
US Peace Corps www.peacecorps.gov
Voluntary Service Overseas www.vso.org
World Bank – Children & Youth Dept.
    web.worldbank.org/WBSITE/EXTERNAL/TOPICS/EXTCY/0,,menuPK:
    396453~pagePK:149018~piPK:149093~theSitePK:396445,00.html
World Youth Congress on Youth & Development www.wyc2008.qc.ca
Youth Action for Change www.youthactionforchange.org
Youth Action Net www.youthactionnet.org
Youth Business International www.youth-business.org
Youth Challenge International www.yci.org
Youth Employment Summit www.yesweb.org
Youth Service America www.ysa.org
Zivildienst www.zivildienst.de

OTHER SCHUMACHER BRIEFINGS

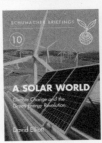

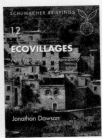

1. *Transforming Economic Life* by James Robertson £5.00

2. *Creating Sustainable Cities* by Herbert Girardet £7.00

3. *The Ecology of Health* by Robin Stott £5.00

4. *The Ecology of Money* by Richard Douthwaite £7.00

5. *Contraction & Convergence* by Aubrey Meyer £5.00

6. *Sustainable Education* by Stephen Sterling £5.00

7. *The Roots of Health* by Romy Fraser and Sandra Hill £5.00

8. *BioRegional Solutions* by Pooran Desai and Sue Riddlestone £6.00

9. *Gaian Democracies* by Roy Madron and John Jopling £8.00

10. *A Solar World* by David Elliott £6.00

11. *The Natural Step* by David Cook £6.00

12. *Ecovillages* by Jonathan Dawson £6.00

13. *Converging World* by John Pontin and Ian Roderick